Honest Grief

By Serenity McLean

Copyright

Published by Dome Tree Publishing
ISBN 978-0-9952721-4-9

DOME TREE
Publishing

Disclaimer

This book is not intended to replace the services of a mental health professional. Grief can be a deep, dark, lonely place. If you find you are not making progress or slip into a clinical depression, definitely get in touch with a licensed mental health professional.

Contents

My Story

Fellow traveller, let me share my story of massing losses. I won't go into great detail, but just enough that you can understand where this guide comes from.

Loss one: my job. It started with being packaged out. I worked for an oil and gas service company in an oil and gas town. When the price of oil plummeted, anyone whose job depended on capital spending was packaged out.

Loss two: one dog. Three days later I had to put down one of my beloved dogs due to cancer.

The area I lived in was economically depressed because of the oil prices and work would be hard to find in my area of expertise. In rising up from these first two losses, I made a decision to change the direction of my career. It would take quite a bit of time for my idea to take off, but everything else in my life was good. I had a very peaceful home and an extremely happy life with my chosen life companion (my mom) and our two dogs. And together we were financially okay. I had hope and resiliency back then.

Loss three: my mom's health. A year later we got the news Mom had terminal cancer. I rose up again from that loss and, while it was difficult and very draining to watch life ebb out of her every day for a year, I was grateful to be home to care for her, and would not do anything differently.

Loss four: another dog. Three months into that last year with my mom, I had to put down a second dog, this time with cancer in her head cutting off her breathing. Knocked down again. Standing up again and carrying on was a bit slower and harder. I began again at the start of the grief road.

Loss five: Mom. She was failing and mid-December we agreed she would go into a hospice. On Christmas Eve, late in the evening and alone, she died. Although I knew this was inevitable, it was devastating. My heart ripped to shreds. So much that was good in my life disappeared with her death. Afterward I felt I sat at death's portal for a long time, wishing I could find a way through that door to the other side where Mom and I would be together again. It took a lot of courage to stand up and walk on. I was drained from the year of letting go of Mom, yet I began again at the start of grief, this time with massive storms of anguish and sorrow.

Loss six: my home. There were no jobs and I couldn't afford to keep my house. I had to sell much of what I owned to move back east to where there was work. There was no choice. While reeling from my mom's death,

I didn't have time to grieve. I got busy and cleaned out her belongings and sold our home. I walked away from the place we shared for over a decade – that place of peace and joy was gone from my life, that place where she sang, "I love you a bushel and a peck," to me from the top of the staircase. I did what had to be done. No time for grieving.

Losses seven and eight: a job and health. During my last couple of weeks in our home, I managed to line up a job and once back east I was going to meet the executives for a final decision. I found out later I was their only candidate. What I didn't realize is that during this time I had a spontaneous subdural hematoma (for no reason, blood vessels began to bleed in my head, and blood pooled against my brain causing massive headaches which I thought was just due to tension). When I arrived at where I was temporarily staying, I finally went to a doctor and discovered how serious these headaches were. Since they were talking surgery, and my head was a total fog, I had to inform the company I couldn't take the job.

Three months later and the blood still had not dissolved. It continued to hurt with any kind of pressure and my thinking remained foggy. I was unable to deal with writing and words. I don't remember much of these days. Dealing with my grief was impossible.

Six months later it was slowly healing, so the doctor decided against surgery, but recovery was very slow as I could expect it to take up to a year to get my brain function back again once all the blood finally dissolved. This meant I was unable to get a job.

After losses in every area of my life, I found myself sitting on the ash heap that once was a happy life. There was no avenue out – no ability to work, and no white knight in shining amour riding in to pick me out of this mess. It was day after day living in the ruins of my life. I had one thing left – my sweet dog Abbey.

Loss nine: Yes, Abbey. Before the end of that first year after Mom's death, my last dog was diagnosed with a brain tumour. She was the only living being in my life. With so much missing, she became the only place for all my love that swirled about and had no place to land. I didn't know if I wanted to stand up again or even could. What was the point? Another loss would just come along and knock me down again. The grief stew seemed bigger than I could take on. This was the proverbial straw that broke the camel's back. It wasn't that one dog's death was huge – it was that the pile of loss was unbearable.

And yet the sun continues to rise, and we are left with no choice but to deal with it. For me, a big source of feeling helpless and hopeless came from the continuing losses that seemed to visit regularly – just when I seemed to be getting on my feet again.

Yes, everybody experiences loss. But I started to feel like Job. I was stunned at the storm that blew into my life then stood in the midst spinning out continued destruction. I called it the loss parade and saw no end to its continued march of devastation – just like the parade of people that came to Job to tell him of more devastation. Not everybody experiences loss upon loss upon loss until it seems too much to bear. But some of us do.

Yes, I know about loss, and I know about how hard the grief road is, especially when you have to start over and over again with an ever-increasing load. I know what it feels like to be knocked over so many times that you just don't want to bother getting up again. All the emotions in this guide I've dealt with over and over again. I know the pain of others kicking you when you're down, often in the name of Christ. I know months upon months of hopelessness. I know the taste of bitterness and pessimism. I know the abysmal loneliness of this dark valley. And I know the hollow emptiness inside. I bring this guide to you from someone who knows the difficulty of finding your way to serenity after loss.

Serenity

Update: After a couple of months of praying that God would not take Abbey, she suddenly improved. She is a normal happy golden retriever as of the writing of this book. I attribute it to God's intervention. This was the first ray of hope after a very long line of losses. It is evidence that loss does not go on forever.

Honest Grief

The word honest can be defined as a free, forthright expression. Many folks facing grief don't feel free to fully express their grief in their own way. Onlookers push their expectations on the griever, telling them how and how not to grieve. They will dismiss your feelings, correct your thinking, judge your actions, and tell you when you should be finished grieving. It takes courage and strength to establish and guard the needed time and space to fully work through all the tumult of grief in an authentic meaningful way.

The word grief comes from the French word grève, meaning heavy burden. Indeed, it can be a heavy burden. It's what we experience when we deal with loss. This can include the death of a loved one, end of a relationship or marriage, loss of health, loss of a job, death of a pet, loss of financial stability, miscarriage, retirement, loss of a lifelong dream, selling the family home, loss of a friendship, loss of safety following a trauma. For some, one loss ripples out to others and you watch your life collapse like dominoes. You're left standing among the ruins.

Onlookers often think grief is a sadness associated with a loss in the present, but you look ahead and all you see is barrenness in all your tomorrows. You are grieving not just for what is gone today, but also what is gone from your future, from every single day for the rest of your life.

In Honest Grief I will refer to the loss of a loved one, but loss is loss. Feel free to replace the words loved one with something that describes what you grieve for.

Probably what you find most surprising is that your grief, even in the early days, doesn't conform to the expected five stages of grief. Instead it's a chaotic maelstrom – you bounce from one emotion to the next. There is no warning of shifting emotions. And there's even less control.

In the depths of grief you deal with a multitude of emotions, from shock, numbness and disbelief to anguish, remorse and longing, and many feelings in-between. While grief is a complex mix of emotions, it also affects your mental and physical person. You might feel foggy in your thinking, slow to process, forgetful, indecisive, unmotivated, unable to think of anything but your loss and memories of your loved one, disinterest in life and the living, and perhaps a lack of trust in yourself and others. Physically you may feel exhausted, sick to your stomach, ache all over, suffer with headaches or migraines, a lack of appetite, a physical pain in your heart, insomnia or sleeping too much, nightmares, clumsiness, and a lowered immunity to colds and flus. It's time to look after yourself and give yourself a break from your schedule as much as possible. Doing so doesn't mean you're feeling sorry for yourself. It means you are doing what is necessary to survive this difficult, demanding time. You are protecting and caring for yourself.

Grief is not simply a bit of sadness.

And that's just the part of grief that occurs within you. You're not alone in this world. Even in grief, people are involved in your life. Unfortunately some will contribute to the pile of things you need to deal with and thankfully some will become pillars of support. Find those people who will listen to you without judging. You deserve the space to express your grief – the pain, the confusion, the hurt, feelings of abandonment, the explosive emotion, and the memories. It's important to surround yourself with people who will give you the time to talk about them and accept your feelings. These are the people who know you are working through your grief, and don't tell you how to do it or when you should be done.

It's Hard Enough Without Other People Piling On

In the not too distant past, when someone died in your family, their body remained in your home until burial. Then the family members wore black for a year as a symbol of their grief. During that year the world expected you to grieve. Unfortunately as a society we've become removed from death, uncomfortable with both the depth and length of grief. I had one person suggest counselling after six weeks because they thought I should be over it. Nowadays your work will give you three bereavement days, then it's, "Let's get back to work and hear no more about your loss." When people said stuff like this to me, I called it grief shaming. These are the crazy things people say to you that leave you feeling angry and resentful or ashamed of your grief.

Because people feel uncomfortable with the depth of your pain, they will say things that reflect a total lack of understanding of loss. These platitudes are born from unease with your pain. They really boil down to an attempt to shame you into conforming to their expectations. They don't want your pain to infect or touch their lives. It's important you do not accept their judgment or imposed shame. I'm sorry, but you will have to deal with these hurts. It's not like you don't already have a lot on your plate.

"Get over it." Or maybe you've heard you need to **"Let go and move on."** Let me rephrase this. "Forget about all your pain and sorrow born out of your love and longing. Drop all of it and move on." You find yourself conflicted between dumping your love on a garbage heap and walking away so you can do grief the way others want, or you can ignore this advice and forge your own path. Choose to be honest with yourself.

"Time heals all wounds." You wonder, *The only thing that can heal this pain is for my loved one to come back, and that's not going to happen.* So since you are not healing, you are left feeling like a failure at managing your grief, or angry this person suggests there is healing. There is no healing for grief. There is only learning to live with it in peace. Don't accept their judgment that longing for your loved one is wrong, or that you must heal from grief.

"It's not so bad. They are with you in spirit." Perhaps this thought helps someone out there, but I haven't met them yet. Somehow they think the physical absence of your loved one is meaningless. And if you can't see that, you're not grieving right. *Shame* When someone says this to me, I think, *Okay people, how is that helping? What bit of air can I hug and hold? How do I laugh with them again? I lived with and communicated with flesh and blood, and that's what I'm grieving. I'm alone. Explain how this is comforting!* One grieving friend's response to this is, "If it's all the same, I want my loved one back." It was this one statement that caused me to deal with resentment on a regular basis. It is not wrong to miss the physical contact with your loved one, and no, their invisible spirit (whether it's with you or not) is not an answer to grief.

"They are in a better place." That may be, but how does that help with the pain of loss you feel today? All you want is to have them back. And now you can feel ashamed that you are so selfish, you would prefer them back instead of them staying in that better place. Don't accept this one. It's perfectly normal to want your loved one back. Together again would be the best thing.

"God doesn't give you more than you can handle." And the similar, **"You're strong."** Well, isn't that special! The thing is, you don't want to handle it. You don't feel strong. You're broken and shattered. You feel you've got nothing left to deal with this ginormous loss. And what if privately you're falling apart? Then what? *Shame*

By saying this, what they are really saying is their life is good and they don't want your grief to infect their happiness. They might as well have said, "So let's just say no more about your grief and loss. Suck it up, princess." They want to shame you into never exposing your grief again. Deep

13

grief leaves you feeling swamped – like you're drowning. There are days you don't get out of bed because it's just too hard. You didn't ask for this loss, or the pile of hard work you're going to have to do to get through it. This platitude just makes light of all that work and all the pain. Ignore this one. Be satisfied you made it through another day.

"Everything happens for a reason." How is this in any way comforting or caring? How are you expected to answer this? "Yup, there's a reason my loved one was ripped from my life, and now I am alone, desperately sad, lonely, and did I mention alone? So I guess because you think there is some universal reason for this death and loss, I shouldn't grieve. Shame on me."

It's quite natural to look around at your shattered life and wonder why it all happened. But the truth is, you may never come to an understanding of why. So telling you there is a reason leaves you feeling ashamed you are too stupid to figure it out. Don't listen to this nonsense.

"They are in a better place." The logic of this totally escapes me. This implies your desire to have them with you rather than dead means you don't want the best for your loved one. What this statement really means is dead is better. There were times when someone said this to me, and I wanted to respond with, "If dead is better, then I want to be dead too," just for the shock value.

This one leaves you feeling ashamed that you long for something apparently not the best for your loved one. Longing to have them back is perfectly normal. Don't accept any statement that doesn't honour your feelings.

"I know how you are feeling." How could they possibly know how your grief feels? You can barely sort out how you're feeling at a given moment. It can change in a heartbeat, from sorrow to anger to resentment to isolation to loneliness – all in the ten seconds following a dumb platitude like this one.

"It could be worse." What? How could it be worse than your life in total barrenness, darkness and destruction? What could be worse than dealing with the anguish of loss for the next how ever long it takes so you can reach a place of serenity? I just don't understand how this can be considered caring and supportive. Death and all the related losses will probably be the worst thing you have to deal with in all your life. Don't accept their opinion here.

"Life must go on." When you're not feeling a part of life and the living, this one just makes no sense. This just dismisses the need for grief altogether. It's as though they said, "You've had your three days off from work. Now you just need to get back to the way you were before."

This comes from someone thinking only of their own discomfort with your grief and wishing to shame you back to being that person you were before death blew a big cavernous hole in your being. Ignore this and forge your own path.

"Count your blessings." Sure, there are always blessings, like the sun came out yesterday, but you may be in no frame of mind to count them when barely making it through the day. What this actually means is it's time to put away the work of grief and suppress your feelings. It's time to be happy whether you are ready or not. When you are mentally and emotionally ready, you will see the good in life again. For now, you are overwhelmed by anger, resentment, sorrow, anguish, searching for your loved one, regret, remorse, loneliness, helplessness, hopelessness, despair, stress and pressure. You may not see the blessings or have the resources to count them. Don't feel ashamed because your gratitude is taking a break.

"At least they had a good life." And you want it to have lasted longer. Does this mean it's okay for a life to end if it was a good life? You're lonely and upset. You miss your loved one and someone says this to you. I guess you are supposed to quit grieving because they lived a good one. There's nothing good about this statement.

"It's for the best." From the viewpoint of someone unattached to your loved one, this may well be how it looks. Maybe your loved one suffered a long battle with a terminal illness. So this could be viewed as a true statement, but it definitely is not a caring one. You are suffering a great loss, perhaps the greatest one of your life. You have a huge part of your heart that has been hollowed out. Almost every aspect of your life has been pulverized. You can't see past the desolation to comprehend this statement. And the truth is the best would be if they were still healthy and alive and with you.

"It's time you snap out of it." So much is wrong with this one. Grief has no prescribed timeline. It's not like you can take your three bereavement days to grieve, then be done with it. Brace yourself. Grief doesn't go away. People who have walked through the deepest part of the valley of loss say grief stays with you for the rest of your life, becoming part of you. Eventually you will find a place where you can live with it and not feel devastated. In the meantime, don't feel ashamed you experience a complex mix of feelings and your grief road is convoluted, rocky and difficult.

Grief is not one of those things you will just snap out of because in every one of your tomorrows, the great chasm of loss will still exist. And you feel can't "just move on" because that would mean leaving behind all those treasured memories with your pain of grief. Unfortunately when you experience loss, the hole in your heart, the chasm in your life, the pain, the anguish, the chaos of emotion, and your love all come as a package – I call all of it **grief stew**. It takes time to get through your grief stew. There will be no snapping out of it.

And the big winner for a dumb thing to say is, **"Those who believe need not grieve."** Wow, really? I know several religious books talk of the reward of reuniting with our loved ones in an afterlife. Unfortunately the ignorant oversimplification is absolutely devastating to the one grieving.

No promise on a far distant future date, no matter how wonderful that will be, removes the deep anguish of loss today. That future promise doesn't lessen the suffering you witnessed as a loved one slowly succumbed to a terminal illness. It doesn't erase the hopes and dreams you had for your future with them. Let's just be really clear. Experiencing grief, even deep, crippling grief, does not indicate a lack of faith.

When you experience loss you have two options. You embrace the entirety of grief stew – the heart hole, the chasm in your life, the pain, anguish, the emotions and your love – and you take the tough journey through the valley of grief to find your way of living with it. There is no cure for grief. Your loved one died. There is no bringing them back. So the hole in your heart and the chasm in your life will remain with you for all your tomorrows. There will be no cure or getting over it like you would the flu. This is a huge amputation. By forging your grief road, you will build a new way of living, a way that includes the hole in your heart and life, and the love in your heart – and that simply takes time and effort. How long? Only time will tell how long it takes to find your new way of being.

This means there will be no end to the grief. There will be an end to the chaos and storms of it, but once loss brings grief into your life, it remains. It changes you. It remoulds you. You will not be the same person you were before. There are massive chunks of you that are gone and you'll never get them back. Choosing to address your grief stew means you are willing to do the hard work of dealing with your thoughts and emotions, even while the storms of grief assail. By doing this work those storms will subside, and you will come to a new way of living in serenity with your loss. All this takes time and effort. Don't let anyone push you into moving on without discovering and accepting your new way of being.

The other option is to skip the whole grief thing and not embrace the grief stew because you fear the pain will be more than you can bear, or because you have been shamed into moving on. You suppress the emptiness, the anguish and thoughts of your loved one. In the long run, this option is more damaging because the thoughts and feelings about loss will linger until you deal with them. Ignoring them can lead to mental and health disorders later on.

If you are still reading this, then you are willing to forge your own road of grief so you can bring your love into your future. You loved this person deeply, and while you will live with a hole in your life during every one of your tomorrows you will also be able to express your love in your future. What an honour to them!

A Bit About Grief

First, there are no wrong ways to feel grief. Everybody's grief stew is their own recipe, with their own unique flavours. There are constructive ways of dealing with grief – and some not-so-constructive ways. Hopefully with this guide you will discover many practical and helpful things you can do to address the tumult of emotions and meaningful ways to express your love.

Many will view your forging your own path through grief as a self-absorbed, narcissistic, needy approach. My guess is those people have never experienced a life-altering loss, or have chosen to not forge their own path to find their place of peace. It will take strength to not allow those judgments and pressures to put shame on your honest grief.

For some, knowing there are better days ahead helps them through the tough days of grief. For many, they can't see beyond their pain to envision the future. It's important to know at the start of this road, happiness or normalness is not today's goal. It may be other people's goal for you, but just making it through this day, this hour, this minute is the goal.

Although it doesn't look like it today, there will come a day when you finally make some form of peace with the loss. You'll have chewed through all the bits and bites of your grief stew, even the tough, grisly ones, and come to a stillness about what has happened, where you can look forward into your future without debilitating emotion. There's still the hole in your heart and the chasm in your life, a huge amputation, but you will have built a new way of living with it. You will have created a new way of being – a new definition of yourself. You'll have found your way to face all those tomorrows. The storms and chaos will calm. Until then, stake out all the space and time you need to walk the grief journey in the way your heart and mind require. The switch from tumultuous sorrow and pain to the serenity and sweetness of remembering won't come overnight. But it will come. You will find peace offers the briefest of visits as a casual acquaintance at first, but over time you will form long lasting relationship with peace and it will become a constant companion.

In our current world there's an unhealthy expectation that life must be completely filled with happiness. Somehow sadness is considered almost pathological. We want to medicate away any symptom or health item that might stop our constant stream of happy. Think about all those drug ads and the happiness portrayed. I know many people love Pharrell Williams' song "*Happy*", but I see it as evidence people actually believe a constant, almost irrational happiness is the goal in life. It seems the message is if you're not so overwhelmed by happiness, then you've failed at life. Or worse (and equally wrong), failed at faith.

Let's be honest. It's quite normal to have times of sadness – even if you weren't dealing with a loss. Life is filled with everyday disappointments. It's an unobtainable goal to expect you will "get over" your grief and never feel sad again. The hole in your heart and life are now with you to the end of your days. Therefore sadness will revisit – and that's not only okay, it's normal. In time, when sadness visits for a spell, you will not be in the midst of the storms of grief. You will come to a place of serenity and a new way of being still with a hole in your heart. And yes, you can be in a place of peace and still have a time of sadness. That simply is your love talking.

Unfortunately, right now your world is void of colour. You know that person can't come back, but it's the only thing your heart wants. The only brightness in your life shines dimly from the past. Today is dark and the future even darker. Right now you live with a never-ending pain that shatters your heart and crushes your soul. You need to know this – you are normal.

Many days I pleaded with God to take me to heaven to be with my mom. We were best friends. We'd lived an extremely peaceful and happy life together much of my life. We chose each other as a life companion. When she died, I didn't want to live on without her. My world fell apart. There was no part of my life that wasn't destroyed – I lost my life-long companion, my laughter-filled home, I had no job as I'd been a caregiver, I had a health crisis that prevented me from working, I had no income, no family, I moved across the country to be where there was work, then found out about my health crisis, and the few things I kept from our happy home together were mostly in storage. I was left alone with nothing around me to hang onto. I felt adrift on an unrelenting sea of loss. The grimy hands of loss gripped every part of my life, squeezing with an incessant pressure. There was nothing left in my resiliency bucket to handle any additional stress. You may feel that way too.

Remember those onlookers who think they know what you are dealing with and think it's their job to tell you how to grieve, what it should look like and how long it should last? Yeah, everybody's an expert except the one grieving. Their words will feel like they are kicking you when you're down. People offer advice that starts with, "You should." "You should call my friend – she just lost a loved one." "You should get out and volunteer."

"You should get a job." "You should be over it by now." Then there is the list of judgments – "So-and-so was over it in a few weeks. What's wrong with you?" "Everybody loses a parent. Move on." "I think you're depressed." "You need a plant." "You need to be with people." "You're not trusting God if you're grieving." Their list of judgments can feel like overwhelming pressure to go in a direction you are not comfortable with or ready for. It's okay that you're not in a place where you can work, socialize, talk about it, volunteer, or whatever it is others think you should be doing. And while it might surprise someone out there, I haven't found any plant made me feel better about my loss.

Have you noticed there's an "I" right in the middle of grief? For once, it is all about you. It's your loss. It's your grief. Therefore it's your journey. Only you know how to walk this road. Only you know when you are ready to take on aspects of normal living again. This is not the time to be concerned about making others feel good or complying with their need for you to be happy. It is about working your way through all the crushing emotions and mental anguish. It's about navigating to a place where you can live in peace with the gaping hole in your heart.

Let me tell you, it takes strength and courage to give yourself the time and space to authentically deal with your grief and loss. If you had expectations that grief has five stages, you're in for a surprise. Grief stew is far more complex and complicated than progressing through five stages. One thing that won't happen is bing, bang, boom, and you're done – happily ever after. Life's just not as simple as a fairy tale.

Be kind to yourself. You are in the midst of the suffering part of "You suffered a great loss." Now is the time to give yourself lots of special care. Don't forget to eat and get plenty of rest. Regularly invest in self-kindnesses like taking a long soak in the bath, or sobbing out your emotions by candlelight. Be gentle in how you see yourself. Grief is hard work many will not understand. Think about yourself as a dear friend suffering. With yourself, be kind, generous, compassionate, tender, patient, protective, accepting, open to fully experiencing your feelings, and to finding your way through the valley of grief.

The point of this guide is to work through your emotions, reflect on your journey, and find things that confirm the significance of your loved one and your relationship with them. This is how you can come to live in tranquility with your loss.

Blessings to you as you forge your own trail.

How to Use This Guide

Many emotions are possible and your journey quickly becomes a convoluted, tangled mess. That's quite normal. It can feel like you are making progress only to be revisited by an emotion you thought you were done with. When you see your journey as this mixed-up passage, you realize the importance of being compassionate with yourself. You'll read it often. *Be gentle and kind. You are learning a new way to live.*

Feelings of Grief

You will find descriptions of three dozen of the most common feelings you may experience in your grief stew mix. There is no right order in which you'll experience them. They are presented in no particular order. The trail you forge may take you on a convoluted journey through this guide.

Your circumstances are uniquely yours. You now find yourself a stranger in a foreign land struggling to survive. While everyone's grief stew is different, we are all human and you will see yourself within the description pages. The most important thing to remember is your feelings – all of them – are a normal part of grief. This tangled mess is truly normal.

Shock   Turmoil   Re-Entry   Serenity

Following each description are some things you can do to help your head and heart address, process and handle the emotions, to capture and reflect on your thoughts and find your own way through this deep, dark valley of loss.

Grief Stew Work and Reflections

The grief stew activities are things to help you through the hard work of grief. It can be difficult. This can be tear-filled work, and you may need time to sort out your thoughts. As you encounter an emotion, give the exercise a try. If you find you're not ready, that's okay. Come back to it another day. Not every day is a good day for chewing on the grisly bits. Some days it's enough to know all of this is a normal part of grieving and you are really okay. Some days getting out of bed really is good enough.

Even if you haven't experienced the emotion described, take a look at the activities. For example, you may not feel numb, but rather a hurricane of emotions. Nonetheless, you may find creating a memory jar to be very meaningful. Take some time to browse through the entire book and mark the things that resonate.

You may not be much of a writer. You don't need to be good. Don't worry about spelling or grammar. Don't worry about finding the perfect word or getting it just right. The meaningfulness of the exercises and the aha moments come from your authentic responses – your genuine thoughts straight from deep inside. Just write how you really feel. Don't censor your thoughts. Just be honest. Then take time to reflect on your responses. It's a good idea to go back and revisit earlier writings often. You will be surprised at what you can learn.

This is your private journal. It doesn't need to seen by anyone. Be comfortable with your deepest, even ugliest thoughts and feelings. They are all legitimate. There's no right and wrong way to grieve, despite what others may tell you.

While dealing with grief, people seem to come out of the woodwork to tell you how you should think, feel, act and for how long. This can feel like a constant pressure to be something you're not, or do something you're not ready for. There will be enough stress in your life. This guide shouldn't be another one. Remember, you are in control of when you work through these exercises. There's no right timeline to grieve, so let your heart and head set the schedule for sitting down to a bit of grief stew. But don't let fear of the pain of confronting your anguish deter you from going through your grief stew work.

Honest Grief Notebook

This book references a FREE notebook that is preformatted for the grief stew and reflection exercises. Go here (http://serenitymclean.com/honest-grief/) to download. You will see a link on the left side part way down. Print on 8.5 inch by 11 inch paper and it is ready to use. Alternatively, you can use a binder with lined note paper, or a notebook to write your notes.

Diamonds

The memories of your loved one are like diamonds. They might be covered in pain right now, but when you shine them up they sparkle their brightness into your days. They really are treasures you want to hold onto – it's part of loving someone who has died. You'll find a number of ways you can keep a connection to your loved one – things that bring memories forward with you as you move through the remainder of your life. Some are public things to be shared and others you will want to keep private.

These activities often result in the creation of sentimental objects or involve participation in deeply meaningful activities that honour the memory of your loved one. Nothing can bring them back. And nothing will fill the gaping hole in your heart, but you can create an environment where they are not forgotten. You loved their physical presence in your life and you will be creating tangible objects you can touch and remember. It's okay if one of the suggestions doesn't resonate with you. There are lots to choose from.

Self-Kindnesses

Dealing with grief will be very demanding. It needs to be tackled a bit at a time as you have the resources to turn and face your stew. You will need to continually find ways to renew yourself. These are the small kindnesses you do for yourself. Take a look in the self-kindness section for more information and a list of ideas to get you going.

Final Words

This section started with a picture of how your grief journey looks over time when you commit to the hard work of dealing with grief and loss. Yes, it's scary and feels like your life is out of control. You feel tossed about, steamrolled over, flooded out or drowning in mountainous waves. But as you deal with those chaotic thoughts and out-of-control emotions, as you invest in yourself with self-kindnesses, the storm winds will begin to subside. When you've addressed all the chaos, pain, anguish and anger, when you've found a way to live peacefully with a hole in your heart and a missing person in your tomorrows, you will come to the place of serenity with your grief. You will have discovered your new way of being.

So today, find the topic you want to address and let's get started.

Shock

It feels like a life-wide numbness, like a ten-ton truck flattened you, or a fog you can't seem to clear. You feel like you're operating on autopilot, or that everything is happening at a distance. You may be aware of things happening around you, but you feel you are not really there. Often this is an early response to loss. It's a protection against the pain. And what a blessing because it can help you get through those difficult tasks associated with a recent death.

Unlike physical shock mental shock can go on for months. You get busy with things that need to be done, and people around you think you are coping so well. But you don't remember most of what has gone on. It's like you weren't even present for most of those shock days. Looking back you have little memory of what occurred.

And then one day you realize, you survived. Somehow you got through those toughest of days. You've taken your first steps on your grief road. There is still a lot of difficult road ahead, but you have proven to yourself that you can cope. Mental shock will recede gradually as you become ready to deal with the deepest parts of grief. Remember, everyone's journey through grief is different. Honour and respect where your heart leads and accept when your mind protects.

On the grief road you may feel crazy, lost, alone, confused, foggy, sad and empty. It seems like there's no end in sight. It may take a lot of time to recover from the mental shock, but the mind has a way of gradually restoring itself. Even when it feels there is no end in sight, know the mind has wonderful recuperative powers. Don't rush it. Allow yourself the time to repair.

You may wish to read about numbness later in this guide. It is closely related to shock.

Be gentle and kind. You are learning a new way to live.

Grief Stew: 15-Minute Grief Space

The pressures of funeral arrangements, death notifications, and conversations with family and friends have left you little time to be alone with your feelings. If you feel the building pressure to let them out, find a quiet, private space where you can be alone for 15 minutes. Think about your loved one that died. If you want to cry, let yourself cry. If you want to scream, then let it out. If you just want to sit in stunned silence, then let the silence be your quiet companion. Take these few minutes to give yourself over to your grief in whatever form it takes. When the time is up, promise yourself you will continue to make time to let out your feelings, but for now there are things that need to be done.

Don't be shy about making time for a grief break as often as you need. This is a way of caring for yourself rather than stifling your emotions.

Reflection On Making Space for Grief

Page 5 in the Honest Grief Notebook

What do you appreciate about shock and what do you find most difficult? What is the impact of making space to grieve? What are your thoughts about when the shock subsides and deep, painful emotions introduce turmoil into your life?

Denial, Disbelief and Aftershocks

Hearing your loved one coming into the room, expecting them home at a certain time, waking up and forgetting they have died, smelling their cologne or perfume and turning to see an empty room, getting two cups out for tea, then remembering you are alone, rolling over in the morning and reaching out to an empty bed, then dealing with the brutal reality they are gone – these are all part of denial. It's hard to grasp the loss is permanent and real. You know they've died, but at the deepest levels it's difficult to accept the hard reality. Fear, confusion, and panic can be a result of the struggle between the knowledge they've died and the deep-down disbelief.

Denial is a defence against experiencing the reeling impact of your loss. It's a way we have of giving ourselves a break from the deep pain. It gives you the time and space to process your feelings without becoming overwhelmed.

Disbelief is very common in the early days as you still live with the habits of a lifestyle with your loved one present. It will take time for those habits to fade. But disbelief is not limited to the first part of your grief road. It can revisit many times in aftershocks. And it's quite normal to experience these, even long after your loved one died. You may go several months, then suddenly you think you hear them and the tsunami of loss rolls over you.

The thing about disbelief is it will dissolve at its own speed. Give yourself time. Disbelief and aftershocks are quite normal. As they dissipate you will discover you are able to slowly turn and face the pain. When you are ready you can pry open that protective shell and deal with your feelings. Don't rush it. Let your heart and mind lead you to those painful places when you are ready.

Be gentle and kind. You are learning a new way to live.

Grief Stew: Life Inventory Part 1

Page 6 in the Honest Grief Notebook

Take stock. In your workbook list what you've lost and what remains. Come back often and add items to both lists as you think of them. (Part 2 of this exercise can be found in the Share and Talk section)

Reflection: On Loss and Retention

Page 7 in the Honest Grief Notebook

How do you feel looking at this list? Do you think it is an accurate view? As time passes what do you notice about each list? In time, when you look back over the changes and additions you've made, what have you learned about yourself and grieving?

Numbness

So you sit there feeling nothing. It's not the same as a normal day when feelings aren't playing a big role. This is a cavernous emptiness. You feel emotionally lifeless – all around you people are feeling something – and you feel absolutely nothing. You're dead inside. You have nothing to contribute to those around you, or to life in general. In fact, you can't relate to those who are feeling. The world seems meaningless. You look at yourself in the mirror and it seems like you are looking at a stranger. You may think you'll never return to normal. You feel like an alien, isolated from the world. You feel alone, and you don't really care.

You may even think there's something very wrong with you for reacting to your loved one's death with numbness. You wonder if this lack of feeling is a reflection of how you really felt about them. Did your love for that person die with them?

Good news. Numbness is a way the mind protects you against an overwhelming onslaught of emotional pain. It's like there is a lake of pain you need to face, but if the dam broke and you had to deal with the rush of water, you wouldn't survive. So the dam has been closed for a time until you are ready. That is numbness.

Just be aware that sometimes the dam can suddenly open up and more water than expected is released. You may deal with a day when the numbness breaks and your emotions come rushing out.

What's important to remember is your numbness has nothing to do with your love. Certainly if you find yourself feeling this way for a long time, or it's impacting your life, you should talk to a licensed mental health professional.

In the meantime be thankful for your mind's protective shelter, even though it can be disorienting. And don't try to elicit emotions just to prove you are still alive. Be gentle and accept your mind is protecting you and accept numbness as a gift.

Be gentle and kind. You are learning a new way to live.

Grief Stew: Reconnect with Yourself

Book yourself an afternoon at the spa or arrange a massage. While getting your treatment focus on the sounds in the room (the relaxing music, the sound of water, etc.). Pay attention to the scents, taking in deep breaths and letting them out slowly. Think about how the treatment feels. Concentrate on relaxing your muscles. Let yourself be in the moment.

Reflection: On Being Present

Page 8 in the Honest Grief Notebook

What are the aspects of numbness you find helpful? What about it makes it difficult for you? What did you enjoy about going for a massage or spa treatment? Why? How did you overcome the challenge of staying present throughout the treatment? Overall was this a positive experience? Would you do this again? What alternative things could you do to connect with yourself? What have you learned from this experience?

Diamond: Start a Memory Jar

Get a pretty glass jar or glass bowl, a fine-point marker and some flat stones. Some people paint the stones in bright colours or the favourite colours of their loved one. When you think of a good story of your loved one, or someone shares a good story, write a short description on one of the stones and add it to your jar. You may want to leave the jar and stones out for family and guests to contribute to as well. Be sure everyone includes their name on the back of the stone.

In time you can decorate your jar with ribbons, photos, paint, or things from places or activities your loved one enjoyed. For example, if they loved the beach and ocean, you could add small shells to the stones. I added flameless tea lights.

Anger

Resentment, anger, and fear are all connected and a normal part of grieving. One perspective on their relationship is that past things lead to resentment, current things lead to anger and future things cause fear. Each is dealt with differently.

For some there is little anger on their grief road. For others there is a lot. Anger can be a reflection of how much you loved the person who died. The energy of anger can carry you through some very difficult days. You may be angry at the person who died, the legal mess, the medical bills, the person who caused their death, your loved one's doctors, caregivers, well-meaning people who say thoughtless and hurtful things, friends who have disappeared, God, yourself for something you did or think you should have done, or the world for continuing to live and laugh. You may find yourself snapping at people for no reason at all, or fuming at a person acting on their company's policy. You may see yourself as being the crazy, angry person. In other words, you're angry in general over the unfairness of their death.

It's okay to feel angry as long as you don't physically hurt yourself or others. The problem comes when you don't address the cause of your anger or vent its building energy. Once it reaches a certain point, it needs to be properly expelled – it needs to be drained. If you let it hang around too long, anger can turn to rage, revenge or bitterness, all of which are destructive. Find a strategy or two to explore and deal with your anger so it doesn't become the defining characteristic of your grief.

Remember, anger is a very normal part of grief, and it's okay to be angry, but don't let it become damaging.

You may also find the related topic Resentment of interest.

Be gentle and kind. You are learning a new way to live.

Draining the Red Energy

Since suppressing your anger can have long-term harmful effects on your health, it's important to find a harmless way to vent some of the energy. Here are some ideas.

Express Yourself

Tell others what you need and want in a clear assertive (nonaggressive) way that doesn't hurt them. For example, you can say, "What I really need is a friend that will listen and not try to fix things. Grief doesn't need a solution, but acceptance and support." If you're concerned you'll say the wrong thing, write it out and rehearse it.

Mindfulness Practices

First find a quiet setting for any of these mindful practices (in your office with the door closed, on a park bench, in your car, even a bathroom stall). The first suggestion is to practise a relaxation or visualization exercise, one where you see yourself releasing energy. Spend some time recalling the details of a positive memory such as a favourite vacation, a relaxing place like the beach, or alongside a mountain stream. Imagine the sounds and smells. Visualize the details and colours of your memory's environment. Practise some deep breathing exercises. Another option is to visualize what made you angry then erase the scene to reveal yourself in a calm state.

Share It

Tell a trusted friend how you feel. Find a friend, a minister or therapist who will listen and not judge. Don't worry about getting it right. Just tell it.

Let It Out

Scribble how you feel on paper. Let your emotions direct the shape of the marks, the force of the pen, the strength of the stroke. You may wish to name your frustrations while scratching out your emotions. When your paper is full or you are done, crumple it up and throw it out. Picture your anger being discarded with the paper.

Write your anger in letters and read them out loud (to the mirror, if you want).

Imagine the object of your anger sitting across from you and tell them what made you angry and why it makes you angry. I've even talked it through with an imaginary passenger in the car.

If you enjoy art, you can use paint or coloured pencil to paint your anger. When done you can throw it out. I liked to tuck it away. If my anger over that incident arose again, I'd pull out this emotion page and paint in my new feelings. When the page was full, or I was finished with the particular provoking incident, I'd file it away in a folder labelled I'm Done With This. You could even put them in the freezer to cool off.

There are a lot of creative ways of expressing your negative emotions. Some paint on their computer, some like sculpting, and some sketching out a comic strip. If you are creative, think about how you can use your creative talents to express your anger. Then get rid of it.

Get Physical

If you find yourself pacing, you may need a more physical means of dissipating the energy. Stomp it out, yell, kick, scream, punch the pillow, or get a punching bag and glove. I know a person who found a cheap source of glass (dollar store). She kept a supply in the trunk of her car. When angry she would find a dumpster and select a few pieces to pitch in as hard as she could. There's something about the sound of glass shattering that can cool an angry heart.

Go for a walk or use another form of exercise (with your doctor's approval, if you have health issues). This can take you away from the provocation as well as help drain anger's energy.

Do Some Good

Get involved with a cause you support (or one your loved one did) to help bring about positive change. This can be particularly meaningful for someone whose loved one died because of violence or drunk driving. Many people have brought about significant changes in society and laws to prevent something similar from happening to another family.

Grief Stew: Red Notes

Page 9 in the Honest Grief Notebook

Identify the reasons for your anger (they may not have anything to do with the thing or person you snapped at), your triggers and things you can change (environment, associations, habits like going for coffee with a particular person). How will you deal with the root cause of your anger? What is the most effective way of finding calm after an angry outburst? How will you know when you need professional help in dealing with it?

Reflection: On An Outside Look at My Anger

Page 10 in the Honest Grief Notebook

Do you see common threads in those things that made you angry? How successful are you in draining anger's energy? How successful are you in dealing with its causes? In the future what strategies will you employ to address anger in your life?

Diamond: Fire Pit Memorial

Build a fire pit with stones gathered from your loved one's property or pretty stones you collect. Or you can have their favourite saying engraved on a capstone, or include a memorial stone with their name and dates. The base could include the handprints of the remaining family pressed in wet cement. Or you can commission a custom-made metal fire pit to be made which includes their name. If they had a favourite outdoor chair, include it with the other chairs around your memorial fire pit.

Resentment

Along with anger you may experience resentment. For me, one of my biggest sources of resentment came from the hurtful things people said off the cuff. I assume they were trying to be helpful, but helpful would be if they brought my mom back, or filled the gaping wound in my life. Short of that there is nothing anyone can do that is actually helpful. Really, it would be great if people learned that. And saying banal things doesn't make it better for the person grieving. In fact, it often just adds to the long list of emotions the griever needs to deal with.

The best thing you can tell people who think they are helping is to keep it simple. Say something like, "There's nothing you can do to make it better. Honestly, I'm good with a simple 'I'm sorry,' or 'I'm thinking about/praying for you.' Please just listen without trying to find solutions because grief has no solution." By listening to you they allow you to let out some of your pain. Try to find people who can be a good listener. For those that aren't so good, explain to them you need a friend who won't judge or tell you what you should be doing.

From one grieving person to you, I know resentment can be a significant part of your journey. I found I needed to write down all the things that brought out resentment, then write out why it hurt and left me resentful.

But resentment can come from other sources. You may resent others who lived on when your loved one died. You may resent how others move on with their lives and seem to not grieve at all. Or how for months you don't hear from those you thought were good friends or even family. And the resulting feelings of abandonment can lead to resentment.

Regardless of whether the source is people or the words they say, you will want to identify those things that cause it, and determine how you will handle your feelings and the source(s).

Be gentle and kind. You are learning a new way to live.

Grief Stew: Dear Person Who Doesn't Get It

Page 11 in the Honest Grief Notebook

Imagine all those people who don't understand you or your grieving. If they were all rolled into one person, what would you like to say to them? Think about all you now find irritating. Write how this "one person" causes your resentment. Write about the results of it and what areas of your life are affected.

For each resentment you listed, go through a forgiveness exercise to develop a commitment to let it go.

Reflection: On Venting Through Letters

Page 12 in the Honest Grief Notebook

Did it help to write a letter to all who make you resentful? Did it help to go through the forgiveness exercise? What will you do with this letter? What have you learned from this experience? Where else could you use this same strategy to express yourself without hurting others?

Diamond: Memorial Garden

Find a peaceful, private place in your yard. If you want to grow plants, be sure to choose a space with some sunlight. You can add a simple water feature to include the sound of moving water. Incorporate some solar lights so you can visit the garden at any time. Think about adding a bird feeder to attract birds into your special space. Be sure to include seating. The centrepiece could be a stone bench with a quote engraved on the seat, or a memorial garden stone with or without a photo, or a special wind chime. Forget-me-nots and roses and plants with your loved one's name (sweet William, lily, black-eyed Susan) are an obvious choice of plant to include, but you can choose flowers in your loved one's favourite colour, or plants that reflect their personality (wildflowers for the free spirited, military colours for the veteran, flowers that will attract wildlife for the nature lover).

It can take a bit of time to build this garden, but you will have years to enjoy it.

Forgiveness

Even the best of relationships contain events and memories that need forgiveness – your forgiveness of your loved one, and their forgiveness of you. You may find while dealing with your grief stew memories of hurt and regret arise. Give yourself permission to forgive – your loved one for the times they failed you, and yourself for the things you failed to do or say. Ruminating on the hurts and failings prevents you from fully dealing with your grief. It can lead to bitterness and prolonged suffering.

Constantly beating yourself up won't change the past. Remember, no one is perfect. You may encounter the need for forgiveness because there was hurt between you and your loved one that remained unresolved. Perhaps they intentionally ended their life, or they abused a substance that took it. Maybe their risky behaviour led to their death, or they opted out of treatment. There may be things they said and did, things they didn't say or do, or they left their estate in a mess. You may need to forgive the health care professionals that cared for your loved one, the people associated with your loved one who encouraged behaviour that ultimately took their life, the person directly responsible for taking your loved one's life such as a drunk driver, friends and family who didn't help during your loved one's illness, or disagreements over end-of-life care, funeral arrangements and settling the estate.

Forgiveness is an action. The result of forgiveness is a feeling of lightness and relief. To get to the good feelings requires work on your part. When forgiving it doesn't mean you agree with and accept what they did or said. Forgiveness acknowledges the wrongs and is an intentional decision to let it go and move on. You pardon their offence without harbouring ongoing resentment. Forgiveness does not mean you no longer believe they did something wrong. You are not assessing the wrongness of their actions, but acknowledging it and your right to be angry, and still choosing to let go of your resentment.

The other part of forgiveness is the forgiveness you give yourself. This is equally important. You will be hampered on your grief road if you are unable to let go of those things you use to beat yourself up with – all those things you regret.

We all have failings. Refocus your thoughts on what you can learn from the circumstances. As you learn to forgive and accept yourself and others, you will discover you are more compassionate. You open the way to living a more fulfilling life and not becoming stuck in the muck of hurt.

The successful process of forgiveness starts with identifying those things that make you feel hurt, angry or resentful. Next decide on whether the benefits of forgiveness are worth letting go of your pain. Forgiveness doesn't mean you can't express your anger or seek justice. It is about not hanging onto your anger. Next you find empathy for the person you are forgiving through understanding them and the context in which they acted. Finding empathy does not imply you've been cured of the hurt, pain or feelings of mistrust. It only addresses your feelings of anger, resentment and possible revenge. Once you've found empathy commit to your forgiveness, and interrupt thoughts of anger with your statement of understanding and forgiveness. Finally, look for the deeper meaning of the forgiveness – the positive impact on your inner being, your ability to cope and success in dealing with your grief.

If the relationship with the person who died was challenging, the hurt and pain you carry can be deep and difficult to forgive. If this is the case, consider working through these feelings with a licensed mental health professional.

Forgiveness takes time. Be gentle and kind. You are learning a new way to live.

Grief Stew: Forgiving Others

Page 13 in the Honest Grief Notebook

Recall the Hurt

This can be what your loved one or someone else did or said, or what they failed to do or say. Identify the action or event causing you anger.

Empathize

Explain the hurtful act from the other side (from your loved one's perspective, or the perspective of the other person causing your anger). Why did they do or say what they did? The intent is not to arrive at the most accurate explanation of their actions. The purpose is to come to a plausible explanation you can live with and to find empathy with that person. For example, "When dealing with enormous pain and facing impending death, my loved one did the best they could to treat me right." Or "Some people are uncomfortable with my pain, so they avoid it by avoiding me." Or "My loved one made their own decisions about drinking. Their death is not the fault of their friends."

Write down your explanation from the other side.

Give the Gift

Can you think of a time when you forgave someone (not just accepting their apology with a quick, "That's okay," but a real, intentional forgiveness)? How did you feel? Forgiveness is the gift that can bring an enormous peace of mind.

Are you ready to write your statement of understanding and forgiveness? Remember, it doesn't mean you think they did no wrong or you can't seek justice. It doesn't mean you can't feel hurt or mistrust them. It means you are going to let go of your right to be angry, your right to treat them equally badly or to get revenge.

Commit to It

When thoughts of anger over this issue arise, are you committed to using your statement of understanding and forgiveness to counteract renewed thoughts of anger or resentment, see it from the other side and let it go?

Reflection: On the Deeper Meaning of Forgiving Others

Page 14 in the Honest Grief Notebook

Give this process time to take hold in your heart. It can take time to really let go. Revisit this page in a few weeks and think about how you feel about this wrong. How do you feel about the person? How do you feel about yourself? Do you see any benefits from letting go of your anger around this issue? What have you learned?

Grief Stew: Forgiving Yourself

Page 15 in the Honest Grief Notebook

Recall the Hurt

Recall what you did or said, or failed to do or say. Identify the thing causing regret.

Empathize

Explain the hurtful act from the other side (from your loved one's perspective or person you feel you wronged). How do you think they would think about the incident? Do you think they would hold this against you? What were the circumstances in which you decided to act that way or say that thing? The purpose is to come to a plausible explanation you can live with. For example, I promised my mom I would be with her when she died, and that she wouldn't be alone. When that didn't happen I felt regret for many months. I came to the place where I could hear my mom say, "I know you love me. I know you held my hand and heard you tell me you loved me that day. I died happy, wrapped in your love. I was not alone because along with your love, God was with me."

Give the Gift

Can you think of a time someone forgave you when you didn't deserve it? How did you feel? Forgiveness is a gift you can give yourself. It is the one thing that will move you past your regrets. Self-forgiveness is just as important as forgiving your loved one and others.

Are you ready to write your statement of understanding and self-forgiveness?

Commit to It

When thoughts of regret over this issue arise, are you committed to seeing it from the other side and letting it go? What will you do next time those thoughts of regret come?

Reflection: On the Deeper Meaning of Forgiving Yourself
Page 16 in the Honest Grief Notebook

Give this process time to take hold in your heart. It can take time to really let go. Revisit this page in a few weeks and think about how you feel about this wrong. How do you feel about yourself? How do you feel about your loved one? Do you see any benefits from letting go of your regret around this issue? What have you learned?

Diamond: Wonderland

If your loved one was a green thumb and enjoyed plants, and you kept one of their plants for sentimental reasons, you can use it for the Christmas tree (or a small table top Christmas tree). Get some starry LED string lights and decorate the plant. It might be a bit unorthodox to have a ficus as your Christmas tree, but who says it has to be a pine? When you turn on the lights, take a moment to remember the good days together.

Self-Kindness

Everyone has a different way of handling stress and grief. Everyone has a different life story, experiences and views of the world. No one sees what your grief looks like when you are alone with it. No one sees the lonely sobs at night, the struggles to get up in the morning, and the pain of adjusting to the aloneness of loss. No one sees the fear or self-recriminations. You were probably unprepared to face your grief. The maelstrom of emotions can be time consuming to sort out and deal with.

Self-kindnesses are the sweet gifts you give yourself. They bring relief. They make room for you to build strength and hope. Of all times in your life, this will probably be the most difficult. Certainly you deserve to be gracious and compassionate to yourself. Gifts of self-kindness are like a sprinkling of sugar, or pretty little wrapped presents that drop into your days to bring a smile or a laugh. Grief is too hard, too draining, too stressful to go through 24/7. These can be little things like taking time to read your favourite comic strip, or something bigger like a vacation. Success in dealing with grief comes from a balanced mix of grief stew work and the sugar of self-kindness.

Regularly choose one of the items on the next pages to do. Check it off when you are done, or take a photo and put it on top of that square as a memory. There's a blank page at the end to add your own ideas.

Be liberal with that sugar!

Be gentle and kind. You are learning a new way to live.

☐ DONE IT!	☐ DONE IT!
Splurge on an afternoon shopping at your favourite stores	Roast some marshmallows at a firepit and make some s'mores
☐ DONE IT!	☐ DONE IT!
Walk an abandoned railway line	Explore a cave or grotto
☐ DONE IT!	☐ DONE IT!
Visit one of the local tourist spots you've never been to	Take in an Observatory or Planetarium show
☐ DONE IT!	☐ DONE IT!
Attend a wolf howl or other nature interpretive event	Try puzzle solving skills in a local corn maze

☐ DONE IT!	☐ DONE IT!
Take a nap in a hammock	Go some place new (new part of town, nearby town, new store)
☐ DONE IT!	☐ DONE IT!
Daydream for half an hour	Let go of a floating lantern
☐ DONE IT!	☐ DONE IT!
Sleep under the stars	Try a new recipe
☐ DONE IT!	☐ DONE IT!
Donate blood	Learn a new party trick

☐ DONE IT!	☐ DONE IT!
Go to the movies with friends	Start a new hobby (playing the piano, painting, model building)
☐ DONE IT!	☐ DONE IT!
Make a picnic and enjoy it in a park	Go to a car show (or boat show or home and garden show)
☐ DONE IT!	☐ DONE IT!
Ride on the back of the shopping cart when returning to your car	Take some time to read your favourite comic strip
☐ DONE IT!	☐ DONE IT!
Go on vacation, even a short weekender	Rent a cottage for a week and explore the new area

☐ **DONE IT!**	☐ **DONE IT!**
Build a snowman	Go to a wine tasting or whiskey tasting evening
☐ **DONE IT!**	☐ **DONE IT!**
Take a horseback ride	Play a round of mini golf
☐ **DONE IT!**	☐ **DONE IT!**
Collect and press some flowers	Frame and hang up your own piece of art
☐ **DONE IT!**	☐ **DONE IT!**
Send a friend a care package	Read one of the top fiction books of the year

☐ DONE IT!	☐ DONE IT!
Go zip-lining	Take a train ride
☐ DONE IT!	☐ DONE IT!
Make a kite and fly it	Spend the morning in a bookstore
☐ DONE IT!	☐ DONE IT!
Take a ride in a limousine	Go outside and sit in the sunshine
☐ DONE IT!	☐ DONE IT!
Hang some Christmas lights in your bedroom, even if it's not Christmas	Visit the local animal shelter

☐ **DONE IT!**	☐ **DONE IT!**
Get a henna tattoo	Go carolling
☐ **DONE IT!**	☐ **DONE IT!**
Bake a loaf of bread	Listen to a new podcast
☐ **DONE IT!**	☐ **DONE IT!**
Binge watch a series on Netflix	Get up early and watch the sunrise
☐ **DONE IT!**	☐ **DONE IT!**
Visit a butterfly sanctuary	Tie die a t-shirt

☐ DONE IT!	☐ DONE IT!
Go to a sports game, local or professional	Go to the local fair and ride the ferris wheel
☐ DONE IT!	☐ DONE IT!
Spend the after-noon on a geocaching treasure hunt	Go to the store and test out the display mattress
☐ DONE IT!	☐ DONE IT!
Run through the sprinkler	Figure out how many grapes you can fit in your mouth
☐ DONE IT!	☐ DONE IT!
Invite a friend for a sleepover	Walk in the rain and jump in the puddles

□ DONE IT!	□ DONE IT!
Have a snowball fight	Draw on your mirror with a whiteboard marker (be sure it's not permanent!)
□ DONE IT!	□ DONE IT!
Lie in the snow and make a snow angel	Spend the afternoon in the library
□ DONE IT!	□ DONE IT!
Watch the sunrise and sunset of the same day	Go to a book signing or reading at a local bookstore
□ DONE IT!	□ DONE IT!
Drink hot chocolate in front of the fireplace	Mismatch your socks and wear them as mismatched pairs

□ DONE IT!	□ DONE IT!
Make a time capsule	Light a candle and listen to some animal sounds (like humpback whales)
□ DONE IT!	□ DONE IT!
Take a photo of your barefoot prints in the sand of a beach	Send a thank you note to someone who has helped you out
□ DONE IT!	□ DONE IT!
Create a Picasso style painting picassohead.com/create.html and save it	Go to a concert
□ DONE IT!	□ DONE IT!
Put on dryer-warmed pajamas before going to bed	Go for a midnight walk

☐ **DONE IT!**	☐ **DONE IT!**
Take a warm spring morning walk and take photos of all the pretty flowers	Visit an aquarium or large fish store for a couple of hours
☐ **DONE IT!**	☐ **DONE IT!**
Visit a winery or brewry	Spend the morning at a local market
☐ **DONE IT!**	☐ **DONE IT!**
Go see a late night movie with a group of friends	Spend a weekend at a five star hotel
☐ **DONE IT!**	☐ **DONE IT!**
Wander around Chinatown or other ethnic area in your city	Watch an outdoor movie or go to a drive in

☐ DONE IT!	☐ DONE IT!
Assemble a 3D puzzle	Send a message in a bottle
☐ DONE IT!	☐ DONE IT!
Dance barefoot in the rain	Go tobogganing
☐ DONE IT!	☐ DONE IT!
Visit a local green-house or nursery	Visit an antiques, thrift, or second-hand store
☐ DONE IT!	☐ DONE IT!
Go to www.jack-sonpollack.org and paint by moving your mouse	Take a walk in the mall

☐ DONE IT!	☐ DONE IT!
Ride in a hot air balloon	Take a long leisure-ly bike ride
☐ DONE IT!	☐ DONE IT!
Go to a local live theater show	Go ice skating
☐ DONE IT!	☐ DONE IT!
Go skinny dipping	Make a pizza from scratch
☐ DONE IT!	☐ DONE IT!
Go to the spa	Change your hair colour (perhaps pink, blue, green or purple)

☐ **DONE IT!**   ☐ **DONE IT!**

☐ **DONE IT!**   ☐ **DONE IT!**

☐ **DONE IT!**   ☐ **DONE IT!**

☐ **DONE IT!**   ☐ **DONE IT!**

Searching and Touch Points

You may find yourself looking for your loved one and seeking a way to remain connected. You may call their name, talk to their photos, or look for them on the street. While I still owned our home, I spent time in my mom's room, touching her things, lying on her bed, and asking God to tell her how much I loved her. I ran my fingers over her photos and spoke to her while watching her on video. If this describes you, you're okay. It is a normal, natural part of mourning. Searching comes from your struggle to believe they are really gone, and from your need to stay connected. With time your searching will fade.

We need connections to our loved one while they lived and we need them even more after they die. Be on the lookout for those little pieces of them you can hang onto. You may not be ready to sort through their belongings, but don't shy away from finding touch points – those objects that allow you to feel connected. Over time you will find things that become your treasures. It could be something valuable, but often it's not. I kept a couple of my mom's favourite T-shirts in my closet – she, mingling with me. I could open the closet and see her shirt next to mine. Some people wear their loved one's jewellery. Some keep items of handwriting. On your journey be open to discovering those things that bring meaning and will keep your connection. It's not weird – it's your love.

Sorting Their Belongings

Immediately following my mom's death, I had to get the house ready to sell. My sister came out to help pack up. I remember the day we sorted Mom's things and she said something about how Mom was reduced to what we would keep and what we would throw away. It just shattered me. It's hard to deal with their belongings. And if you don't have to, don't deal with it until you are ready. It remains one of my regrets that I didn't have more time.

Take your time in sorting your loved one's belongings. Unless circumstances dictate, it doesn't need to be done right away. You will do so when ready. Don't force it. And don't think it needs to be done quickly. You want to spread it over time to ensure you make good decisions. You don't want to regret decisions made in haste.

Be gentle and kind. You are learning a new way to live.

Grief Stew: Who Is This Grief?

Pages 17–20 in the Honest Grief Notebook

Grief is going to be your companion for the rest of your life. In time your relationship with it will change. One way of coming to an understanding of that relationship is to think about who is your grief. What does your grief look like right now? Use coloured pencils or markers to draw it (or cut out magazine images that represent it). Is it a black hole with big boulders dropping through the darkness? Is it a broken heart alone and weeping? Do this exercise again every few months. You'll be surprised at the changing nature of grief and your relationship with it.

Reflection: On Representing Grief

Page 21 in the Honest Grief Notebook

What do you think about your representation of grief? How has it changed over time? What is the significance of those changes? What have you learned from drawing grief?

Diamond: Memory Touch Points

Take photos of the objects or places you feel are a connection point or evoke fond memories. Print the pictures and on the back of each describe the connection you and your loved one shared with these objects/places, your feelings, and the memories they trigger.

Regret and Self-Reproach

Regret is defined as missing very much or feeling sorry. And self-reproach is disapproval or rebuking of yourself.

People often feel regret over some aspect of how they handled their loved one's death. It could be something you did or something you think you should have done. Or it could be regret over something that happened in their last days or moments. It could be as small as something we said that may have hurt them, or something we failed to say. There is no way to go back and change or undo those things we regret.

If you were a caregiver, you may question your decisions about choosing a doctor, or treatment or getting an early diagnosis. If they died suddenly, you may question if you should have pushed harder regarding their behaviours that contributed to their death (substance abuse, poor diet, etc.). Maybe in the busyness of everyday living, you didn't make quality time with them. You may wish you'd worked less, went on more date nights, played ball at the park, attended your son's games or your daughter's recitals. You wonder if you showed enough love and support. You may have a whole list of I-could-haves – I could have called more often, I could have loved more openly, I could have been less strict, I could have stopped him from going out that night, and on and on. Like the ticker tape at the bottom of the news channel screen, regret can be a constant feed of self-reproach.

Take a step back. This perspective of events is really just one lens through which you can view what happened. Just because that's what your ticker tape says doesn't make it true. For example, you may be questioning your decision to move your loved one into long-term care or hospice. At the time you put a lot of thought and consideration into making that decision, but after your loved one dies, all that consideration is forgotten. You question if it was a good decision and whether you acted in a good, kind way. Stop and consider this. This one decision is one small part of years of life with your loved one. This one decision does not define your relationship. Your intention was to do the best you could for them. Remember all that went into making the decision. Ask yourself, will you allow this one well-considered decision to define your relationship?

For me there is the regret I wasn't present when my mom died. I promised her she would not be alone, and yet she died alone in her hospice room late in the evening of Christmas Eve. I had asked the nurses to tell me when her time was close, but they didn't. And she died alone. There is another deep and painful regret that for me is something I have never spoken about, and probably never will, yet the regret and self-reproach is sometimes overwhelming. These feelings need to be faced and dealt with. It's just part of the emotional work of grieving.

People are quick to say, "It's not your fault," and "You shouldn't feel guilty." But if you're like me, your inner person screams, "Stop telling me how to feel!" Most often your feelings of guilt and regret don't mean you are guilty of some wrong. Our irrational brains like to find something to feel guilty about and then the self-reproach becomes consuming.

Know these feelings are a very normal part of grief, and it's quite valid to feel that way. Reject any statement that says you shouldn't feel regret. You do, so it's a part of your grief journey. While it's normal you will need to deal with it. If you find the self-reproach too consuming, find a good counsellor or support group to talk through it.

You will need to identify your thoughts of regret and self-reproach. If they go unnoticed, they can swirl you down into the bottomless pit of despair and isolation. Admit you have these thoughts, and examine their rationality and logic. Think about whether you did the best you could at the time. Then acknowledge it. Accept that in grief your brain can be irrational. Forgive yourself (see the section on forgiveness) and move forward with a new attitude toward yourself. Replace the regret with a positive response. For example, when I say to myself I wasn't there when she died as I promised, I respond with, "I was there for many, many hours every day, even when she no longer was aware of me."

Figure out what you learned and what lesson you will take with you. In time you can use what you've learned to help others. And finally, consider what your loved one would say if you explained your feelings of regret. What would they tell you?

Be gentle and kind. You are learning a new way to live.

62

Grief Stew: My Regret, My Response

Page 22 in the Honest Grief Notebook

Take time to fill in one of these worksheets for each of your regrets. You can print additional pages if needed. Revisit these pages as often as you need, so you can remember your answers to your regret and see how far you've actually come. Here are the prompts for the worksheet.

My regret is

If I told my loved one of these feelings, they would say

I forgive myself because

When I have these thoughts, I will remember

Reflection: On Dealing with Regret

It can take awhile for your response to carry more weight than your regret itself. How do you feel about your progress in dealing with regrets? What have you learned from this experience? What will you do with what you've learned?

Page 23 in the Honest Grief Notebook

Diamond: A Letter from the Other Side

Page 24 in the Honest Grief Notebook

Think about things since your loved one died. Think about how things are going now and how you're handling their death. Imagine you are your loved one – what would they say to you right now? Write out the letter they would write to you, if they could. Read it if your regret or self-reproach needs a little help.

Remorse and Guilt

The word remorse comes from the word bite. It's interesting it's defined as a gnawing distress arising from guilt for past wrongs. Guilt is a feeling of deserving blame for your offences.

There's nothing that can prepare you for the finality of loss. You may have actually made an error in judgment you feel cost your loved one their life (like failing to take their illness seriously and getting medical help quickly). It may be a bad decision you made that led to their death (like driving drunk, causing an accident and their death). There are an endless number of things you can feel guilt and remorse about, and there are no tomorrows in which you can make it right. You now need to find a way of living with the fact these things can't be changed.

If you really feel you owe your loved one an apology, you may feel stuck reliving that apology over and over again for the rest of your life. You may think that is the required punishment for your failure. Remember you are human, no better or worse than anyone else. How hard would it be for your loved one to see you living in this endless cycle of remorse, guilt and self-punishment?

Remorse can be a normal part of grief, but you don't want to be stuck with the condemnation of that ticker tape for the rest of your life. It's important to face these thoughts head on and find a way to feel you have settled the matter. Remorse and guilt can become a burden that drags you into a deep depression. If you have moved into a clinical depression (feelings of suicide, engaging in self-destructive behaviours, difficulty accepting the loss, or no easing of grief emotions over time), please seek the assistance of a licensed mental health professional.

You may find the section on forgiveness helpful.

Be gentle and kind. You are learning a new way to live.

Grief Stew: Pyre of Remorse

There is an art to life in determining what you hold onto and what you let go. Deal with the issues causing you remorse and guilt and then definitely let them go. One option is a holiday season tradition of starting the New Year with letting go of your remorse from the past year. Light a fire in the fireplace or fire pit. Write down your remorse and guilt from the past year, and then throw them into the fire. Watch them burst into flames and quickly disintegrate to ashes. This is a great way to get a fresh start. But there's nothing saying you must wait until the end of the year. You can do this anytime you are ready to let go of the negativity.

Reflection: On Burning Your Remorse

Page 25 in the Honest Grief Notebook

How difficult is it to deal with remorse and guilt? What thoughts and feelings did you have as you watched the paper burn? What have you learned from this experience? How will this experience impact how you manage your relationships with others going forward?

Diamond: A Photo and Note Immortalized

Do you have a special note written to you from your loved one? Or perhaps a poem they wrote? If you don't have the skills yourself, there are businesses where you can send a scanned copy of your loved one's words (in a note or card) and a special photo of the two of you together. They will transfer the image to a canvas and add your loved one's handwritten words on top. Search for handwritten sentiment. Or if you are a bit adventurous, you can print a photo and their writing, and transfer it to a canvas yourself.

Deep Longing and Yearning

There is immense pain and agony when the reality of loss comes to its fullness. As the shock, numbness and disbelief fade, this pain can bring with it a deep longing for our loved one and a yearning for things to return to the way they were. The depth and power of this deep ache can leave you devastated. It can result in dizziness, heart palpitations, difficulty breathing, a feeling of choking, headaches, backaches, neck aches, nausea, diarrhea and fatigue. The physical symptoms usually pass in time.

Give yourself time to say all you need to say and feel all you need to feel. Don't cut off these most painful feelings. You may feel an increasing need to just let it all out. Do it! Sobbing your heart out can be very cleansing and restorative. These emotions burn like red coals deep inside and need to be released so they don't damage you. Like burning coals, longing and yearning can last for a long time. Even when they pass, these emotions can return for frequent visits. Let them in.

Yearning and longing are a very normal reaction to the loss of a loved one. Don't feel ashamed you have these deepest of feelings. They are born of the deep love you have. Your heart is broken into pieces. It needs to fully feel its loss before it can pull itself together again. These feelings are a reflection of your heart trying to find its way to peace.

Have you heard of elephant graveyards? When an elephant dies, the other elephants will gather around and touch their dead companion with their trunks. They stand still and just fondle their loved one. Eventually they continue on their life journey. But every time they pass that area, they return to their loved one's bones. And quietly they gently touch what remains. They still grieve their loss. And they don't forget.

It's very normal to long for your loved one. It's normal to want to find a way to touch them again. Allow yourself the comfort of finding meaningful connections to them. Your wounded heart will appreciate it.

You may wish to read about anguish and acute sorrow, a more intense emotion, as well as searching and touch points in this guide.

Be gentle and kind. You are learning a new way to live.

Grief Stew: Loss Timeline

Page 26 in the Honest Grief Notebook

What are the big losses you've lived through in the past? Take a moment and create a timeline of your losses prior to the death of your loved one. Think about all the beings (animal companions, childhood friends and loves), jobs, and places. Write the losses on the left side of the line. Take a moment to honour your losses – light a candle, if you like. On the right side add the things you've gained from the losses you've lived through.

Reflection: On Past Losses

Page 27 in the Honest Grief Notebook

Consider your loss timeline. You've experienced losses before. Perhaps your previous losses have not been as significant as your loved one dying. Is there anything that strikes you as you reflect on this timeline? Do you see resiliency and strength or something different? What have you learned from your past losses? How could you apply this to your current situation?

Diamond: Create a Music Video

Did your loved one have a favourite song? Have you seen music videos on the Internet that aren't the official video? Often it's the lyrics against a backdrop of different images. Create your own video of their favourite song and share with friends and family. You can use images of places they loved, things they loved doing, and images of them.

Anguish and Acute Sorrow

Anguish is defined as extreme pain and distress. Sorrow is a deep distress and sadness over the loss of someone or something loved.

If you have not cried, that's okay. That's part of your unique journey. You may be holding back the tears for fear if you open yourself up to letting them out, the dam will break loose and there'll be no end. You may be concerned about someone hearing and trying to step into your private grief space. Know it is a human way of releasing the tension and venting some of the sorrow. It can be a significant part of healing. Consider it a gift and if fear is preventing you from letting out your emotions, have faith this is a healthy part of grieving. Allow yourself to open it up and embrace it

Your heart is broken into what seems like too many pieces to fix. You feel hollowed out inside, as though nothing remains. When in deep sorrow groaning, wailing, sobbing grief is just a heartbeat away. In a moment you find yourself falling apart all over again. A friend told me something I think is very true. The deeper you loved, the deeper you grieve. And now the object of your love will no longer be there to share a laugh, a hug, a song, a dance, a movie or a cup of tea. This is what I mean by an empty chasm in your daily life – a deep, bottomless pit that was once filled with their life and their presence.

When you encounter acute sorrow on your grief road, it can hit you with the force of a freight train. It is painful, and the most common reason some shy away from that road. It is scary because you feel like you are drowning in this excruciating emotion. You can find yourself wailing, sobbing, howling, keening, bawling, lamenting or yowling and you don't know how long it will last. Then once you allow it to express itself, you fear it will never end. You think the only possible outcome of this kind of pain is a permanently shattered, broken you. It's tortuous and terrifying.

Despite the pain of sorrow, it is healthy to let those deep grieving emotions out. Some cultures are very good at doing this. But for others it can make people very uncomfortable. I remember people called me depressed. One said I should have moved on after six weeks. But one dear friend told me to cry as much as I needed. He said it was unhealthy to not deal with those feelings and emotions. I'm glad I listened to him.

And don't be afraid to fully express sorrow. There may be a lot of emotion to let out and you may find yourself in a season of agony. It's much like a pressure cooker. In time you will realize the benefits of releasing your heartache.

While the season of deep sorrow will pass, there are still days, and moments sorrow comes to visit for a spell. And that's okay. The hole in your life is still there. Give yourself space and permission to walk with sorrow for awhile.

Be gentle and kind. You are learning a new way to live.

Grief Stew: How's Your Heart?

Page 28 in the Honest Grief Notebook

Notice this question isn't, "How are you doing?" Instead, "How's your heart?" gets right to the heart of the matter. This might be a question you ask yourself several times while travelling your grief road. It's a great way to measure how are really doing. Take a moment to consider, how's your heart?

Reflection: On Going Deep

Page 29 in the Honest Grief Notebook

Have you measured your state based on your heart before? Is this a better measure for how you are getting through your grief stew than, "How are you?" Could it be a good measure for how you get through life in general? Why or why not? What have you learned from measuring how your heart is doing?

Diamond: Who Is Your Loved One?

Page 30 in the Honest Grief Notebook

If you met someone today who didn't know your loved one, what you tell them? What stories would you share? How would you describe them? Paint a wonderful picture of your loved one with words, with sketches, with photos, create a word board, or record your thoughts on video with your smart phone (write down where you saved the video). Tell about the person and character of your loved one.

Nightmares

Initially you may not dream at all. But as the numbness and shock wear off, you may experience painful and upsetting dreams about death and dying. Imagery in your dreams can include injury, death, suffering, graves, ashes, corpses, funerals and coffins. In these dreams people and animals are wounded and living things are hungry or thirsty.

Your dreams can reflect not only your loss, but also your concerns for the future. You may dream about being trapped, unable to move, restrained or being carried away. When dealing with loss and grief, you didn't want your loved one to die and now you may feel trapped in this horrible valley of death. In your dream things may appear foggy, murky or unclear, suggesting you can't see your way out of your current situation. The dream environment may appear messy, crowded, chaotic or under construction – a reflection of the messiness or upheaval of your situation. Some dream of rain, snow, ice or sleet – these bad weather images may suggest unshed tears or perhaps fear.

My first nightmare went something like this. I was walking along a sidewalk, alone on the street even though it was midday in a normally busy section of town. There were no other people and no cars, parked or otherwise. The streets were empty of life, except for me.

All the walkways were under construction, but there were no construction workers, no progress being made. I wasn't able to open my eyes more than a crack to see where I was going. I came to a "T" in the road and crossed the street. The day was bright and clear, but I couldn't open my eyes to see.

I hoped the other side wouldn't be under construction. When I stood on the other side, I heard frantic banging on a window from a nearby building. I strained to open my eyes and see what all the banging was about. And then I was attacked from behind. My arms were trapped as my clothes were ripped off. I was so scared, I couldn't utter a sound. I finally got out a scream and I awoke to my desperate cries.

Although terrifying, dreams and nightmares are a normal reflection of the state you find yourself in while dealing with the pain of grief. Looking at my nightmare, you can see a lot of my grief stew. I struggled with being alone (vulnerability), being blind (can't see a way out), everything under construction, but no progress being made (life in shambles and unable to move on because of circumstances), crossing the street (a change in life's direction), unable to get away (fear I can't get out of this current situation), laid bare (feeling exposed, a fear of being judged), and trapped (constrained to dealing with grief and loss with no escape).

You too may experience terrifying nightmares and disturbing dreams that add emotional strain to an already stressful time. Just know dreams are your mind's way of processing a situation you find incomprehensible. They are a way for the hidden parts of your mind to tell the conscious parts something important. The dream may be related to something you've seen or thought during the day, even something brief. Or it could be related to something you feel is unresolved, like feelings you haven't dealt with. Unresolved emotion expressed as nightmares can be quite common with children.

Bad dreams are simply your mind's way of dealing with the stress of your situation and are an attempt to figure a way forward. Not every dream has meaning, but if you experience a particularly unusual or disturbing dream, you may want to reflect on what your mind is trying to tell you. Dreams, even bad ones are a normal part of grief. View them as an opportunity to gain insight into your internal being. They can clarify the things you still need to deal with in your grief stew.

Be gentle and kind. You are learning a new way to live.

Grief Stew: The Slow Walk

Nightmares can be quite disturbing, even after we awake. The emotions can linger for a long time afterward, even days. Take a slow walk through the park. Be fully present for the entire walk. Being present means having your focus, thoughts, all five senses, feelings, attention and energy directed on this walk. Take your time to really look at the trees, their shape, the texture of the bark, the shininess of the leaves, and the structure of the veins in the leaves. Listen to the birds in the trees and the squirrels chattering. Smell the pine trees, the grass and the moist earth from the dew. Sit for awhile on a bench and watch as others walk through the park. Be very attentive to your surroundings. If it is winter, consider walking through a large greenhouse or indoor garden. Psychology studies suggest when we see lots of green and blue, we experience an increased sense of peace and serenity.

Grief Stew: Dream Log

Page 31 in the Honest Grief Notebook

For those really significant dreams, you may wish to record your dream and its meaning. It can reflect what is most difficult for your mind to deal with and clarifies the areas where you need to focus your attention.

Reflection: On Being Present

Page 32 in the Honest Grief Notebook

How did your slow walk make you feel? Was it hard to stay focused on your five senses in the environment? Was it difficult to intentionally remain in the moment? Is there anything you would do differently next time? Is this a strategy you could use to deal with other kinds of stress or distress? What have you learned from this experience?

Reflection: On Your Dreams

Page 32 in the Honest Grief Notebook

What have your dreams told you? What have you learned? What action will you take?

Diamond: Star Map

If you are a bit geeky or your loved one was, you may like a star map of the night sky from the moment your loved one died, or was born or any other special date. You can order one from https://www.thenightsky.com. Or if you wish to make your own, go to http://www.heavens-above.com/main.aspx and select Interactive sky chart to generate the map.

Abandonment

Not everyone experiences feelings of abandonment, but these feelings may come from a couple of sources. There are friends you thought you could lean on who disappear. You never hear from them. You wonder if they think grief is like the black plague. When their friendship and support is most needed, they aren't there for you, and you might begin to feel abandoned, particularly if this person is someone you enjoyed a close relationship with.

Perhaps the death of your loved one left you in a legal or financial mess. Maybe you are left to raise a young family on your own. Or perhaps you enjoyed a happy life together and their death has shattered it. This can leave you feeling abandoned. While they may not have had any control over their death, you can still feel alone.

These feelings can be deeply painful because you feel wounded. You may feel you're worthless and invisible. By no choice of your own, you've been thrown into aloneness. You feel rejected and betrayed. Abandonment often leads to feelings of inadequacy. It's okay to mourn the loss of relationship and support no longer present in your life.

The problem is abandonment can lead to paralyzing fear and self-loathing. Yes, something you relied on is no longer part of your life. While you grieve this loss, take some time to be proactive in dealing with these feelings. Like so many emotions in your grief stew, while you're justified in feeling them, you need to address the source of those feelings so they don't take over and define your life.

Be gentle and kind. You are learning a new way to live.

Grief Stew: Getting a New Perspective

Page 33 in the Honest Grief Notebook

List all the people you feel have stepped away from you. For the next few minutes, imagine you are an outsider looking in. Now think about their action from this different point of view. Without judging the wrongness of their action, can you think of an explanation for their behaviour that doesn't involve you? For example, one explanation could be that several worrisome issues have cropped up for them and rather than add to your burdens, they've stepped back. It doesn't need to be the correct explanation, just a possible one that allows you to feel empathy for them. Beside each name add your empathetic explanation for their actions. When your feelings of abandonment arise, review these empathetic statements.

Reflection: On You

Page 34 in the Honest Grief Notebook

Today is a good day to establish some positive, life-promoting thoughts. It seems lately you've given a lot of thought to what you dislike about your life – all the grief stew stuff, right? What do you like about yourself? What does your decision to open your heart and mind to your grief and deal with your grief stew say about who you are? How do you feel about your empathetic responses to your friends' actions? Can you find forgiveness and let go of your feelings of abandonment?

Toxic People

Toxic people are those who by their words or actions add more pain and difficulty to your already difficult grief stew. They presume they know "better," and correct your behaviour, your thoughts, your beliefs, your choices and your grief. They ignore boundaries and push their judgments on you, yet seem to have no idea of the pain and hurt they cause. They dispense their wisdom, but fail to accept any. They are always right and even when shown they are wrong will continue to argue they are right. And when they are unsuccessful in controlling you, they quickly shift to becoming a victim. You see them coming and it looks like a tornado of garbage intent on dumping more pain and misery on your already full plate. It feels like they are kicking you when you are down and have no resources to effectively cope with them.

This was one of the hardest things for me while struggling with every increasing loss. I quickly tired of hearing how my choices were wrong. This person didn't know me well, but somehow felt the right to correct – often in the name of Christ. I was angry this person felt the right to correct my grief.

I can tell you what didn't work. When explaining why they are incorrect a toxic person will take offence. When not responding at all – they will find fault in your noncommunication. When distancing yourself – they will exaggerate and find fault in cutting yourself off from "everyone."

Be gentle and kind. You are learning a new way to live.

Grief Stew: Dealing with Toxic People

You can try setting boundaries diplomatically by saying something like, "I prefer to handle my grief my way," or "I'm good with how I'm handling my grief," or "It's important to me to take care of my grief in my own way." These statements shine a light on the fact you are a responsible adult making your own decisions. If they persist, keep restating these are your decisions to make, these are your choices and this is the way you want it.

You can add a thank you in a firm tone at the end of the sentence to indicate the topic is closed, and you will not discuss it further. Socially aware people should understand and back off. For those toxic people that are not, change the topic. If that fails, walk away. Not everyone is worth the effort of a continued struggle. Your peace of mind is extremely important while you deal with a multitude of very difficult emotions. You simply can't afford this person adding to the turmoil. If you need to distance yourself, then do so.

Watch for my new book coming soon called *Supporting Honest Grief*. If you value the friendship, you can try giving them this book to help them understand what you need and don't need from their friendship.

Loneliness

The loss of a loved one leaves a gaping hole in your life. You're left yearning for them. You want them back. You miss them. You need them, but they are not in your life anymore. It is quite normal to miss them. You will be lonely for them, for their physical presence walking through your days. This is the loneliness of life without your loved one.

Then there is the loneliness of the grief road. It is your road to walk and often grievers feel quite alone on the journey. You are the only one who knows what it feels like to carry your grief. You are alone in knowing all the threads and ties of your life and love with the person that died. You are the only one who knows the details of that story of love. Only you know how deeply your life has been altered by their death.

You can feel loneliness because those around you don't seem to understand your pain, or because you don't want to grind through your grief in front of others and turn into a blubbering mess. You may feel alone because others think you're handling it well and you are ashamed to let them see the truth. It's common to think nobody wants to hear about your pain anymore. You may think, "It's a happy family event so I can't bring my sorrow," (and sometimes you think you and sorrow are so attached you can't attend that family event without it). You look around and everyone else seems to be doing so well, you think you just need to suck it up. For one of these reasons or one of your own, you feel you are walking the grief road alone.

Telling someone of your feelings of loneliness can help enormously. It took me several attempts to find the right person, someone kind, loving, nonjudgmental, understanding and accepting. I encountered a number of people that left me hurt more before I found a few that held my hand while I wept over my loss, and laughed with the happy memories, and through it all didn't judge my grief stew. Look for that person who knows you for the wonderful person you are. Tell them how lonely, disconnected and lost you feel. Don't assume they know because you are probably doing a great job at hiding it. You'll be surprised by the sweet relief that comes when you hear someone say, "I understand. It is a lonely road. Can I walk awhile with you?"

Did you notice I reached out to several people before I found the one person who didn't judge, or tell me God is with me so it's wrong to feel alone, or some other inadequate response? When I needed to reach out, these people had the credentials of good support because of who they are.

Mistakenly I thought these people would be there for me, but they weren't. Some were incredibly judgmental, some disappeared and I was left even more alone. But I continued to reach out and eventually found a number of really good, supportive friends. So if you reach out to someone to explain your loneliness and all they give you are platitudes, regroup and try again with someone else. It may surprise you who walks this road with you.

If you simply have no one in your life that will help reduce the loneliness, then find a grief counsellor or support group. They certainly understand the loneliness of grief.

Be gentle and kind. You are learning a new way to live.

Grief Stew: Connection Points

Page 35 in the Honest Grief Notebook

When ready to reconnect with the world, think about things you would be interested in doing with your friends and list them in your notebook. Take some time to list all the points of connection you enjoyed with others before your loved one died. There may be a number in there you feel are no longer a good fit. For example, if your spouse died, a couples' group may not be where you want to spend your time as it could be difficult to be surrounded by happy couples.

Now consider alternative activities you would find interesting – perhaps a book club, choir, gardening group, sports group, leagues such as ping pong, bowling, pub darts, clubs such as photography, biking and hiking, a night class, a church ladies' or mens' group, a Bible study or grief support group. Include your new ideas on the list and explore the opportunities in your area to get involved. You may need to push yourself a bit to get back out with friends. Organize a movie night, a coffee or lunch with a friend or few. Just let go of your grief for a few hours and enjoy the banter of people. Try getting out socially once every couple of weeks at first, and increase the frequency as you become more comfortable.

Reflection: On Connection Points

Page 36 in the Honest Grief Notebook

How did it feel to reconnect with friends? How do you feel about the loss of items on your list that no longer fit? What did you enjoy about trying a new activity? What were the challenges? What have you learned from this experience?

Diamond: Update Letters

Page 37 in the Honest Grief Notebook

Write letters to your loved one. In the first letter or two, openly express whatever feelings you might be experiencing. Don't censor yourself. If you feel angry, lonely, depressed, fearful, happy or relieved, say so. The key is to allow yourself to say what's on your mind and in your heart. Next, you may wish to write a letter of gratitude. Let them know what you appreciate and what you've been grateful for throughout the years.

You can maintain this connection by writing update letters as time passes – much like you would for someone living on the other side of the country. I used my mom's stationery to write to her. It was just another connection point.

Every now and again, open and read your letters.

Solitude

This is different than isolation (where you feel cut off from others and as a result feel lonely and alone). Solitude is when you feel a need for time alone to make friends with yourself, be by yourself and withdraw from the pressures of life. This is quite normal, especially if you are an introvert to begin with. For those of us who feel drained by social situations, pushing us into them while grieving is not helpful. (You may want to read *Quiet: The Power of Introverts in a World That Can't Stop Talking* by Susan Cain if you want to understand the reality of life for an introvert in today's society.)

I often said my bucket is empty. I had no resources to deal with stressful situations and for me, meaningless social situations would just drain away the resources I needed to deal with my grief. Unfortunately I was in a situation where I had to push back hard to make a space of solitude where I could find the peace and quiet I needed.

Choosing time alone is a reflection of your need to get in touch with your feelings and do the work of addressing grief. Much of your dining on your grief stew will be done in solitude. It's hard work. It requires time to think, time to reflect on yesterday, today and tomorrow. It is in solitude you will figure out your new way of being. When ready you will reconnect and give that developing new you a chance to really live.

Our society isn't comfortable with death, so the messiness of grief is not welcomed. Give yourself permission to make solitary time to comfortably deal with your feelings and emotions. It's really a normal part of grief. You need this time. Take it without shame or guilt. You need to piece yourself back together again.

Be gentle and kind. You are learning a new way to live.

Grief Stew: 4-Day Challenge

Pages 38–41 in the Honest Grief Notebook

Set aside 15 minutes each day for four days. Each day write your deepest emotions and thoughts about your loss. Really let go with how you really think and feel. Don't worry about sentence structure, grammar, spelling or punctuation. Just express what is on your heart and mind. Expressive writing is not so much about what happened, but focused on how you feel about it. For 15 minutes keep your pen on the paper and writing. If you run out of things to say, then repeat what you've already said, or let your pen slowly draw a line across the page until you have more to say. If you come across a subject you feel you can't write about because it would push you over the edge, then stop. So, write about how this experience of loss and grief has affected you.

When the time is up, reflect on what you've written.

Reflection: On Expressive Writing

Page 42 in the Honest Grief Notebook

Two weeks after you've completed this exercise, reflect on your life. How do you feel? How do you act? What have you learned from this experience?

Diamond: Chat Over Tea

Be intentional and commit to some time to chat with your loved one. No, you will not actually talk to the dead. Imagine your loved one has joined you for a cup of tea or coffee, and spend those few minutes talking about how you are doing and how things are going. Say those things you wished you'd said while they were still alive. After speaking give yourself some time to sit quietly in the peace of the moment.

Helplessness

One source of feeling helpless is watching your loved one die and not being able to do anything to stop it. If your loved one was diagnosed with a terminal illness, they switched from fighting to live to letting go of life. It can be a long, drawn-out process. At some point you had to let go as well. No one has a choice. They were going to die and you were helpless to stop it.

The feeling of helplessness comes from a lack of control. Even after your loved one dies, you are forced to accept the hole in your heart and the chasm in your life. Helplessly you bury your loved one. Helplessly you return home to face a life without them. You have no control over the appearance, the strength, the duration or the predictability of your grief. You didn't ask for any of these changes to your life.

If your loss is associated with a disaster or traumatic event, it can burst your sense of safety and security. You're left feeling vulnerable and without control. Life becomes terrifying and you are left feeling paralyzed by fear. If this is the case, consider seeking the help of a licensed mental health professional.

Identifying how you have control can help reduce feelings of helplessness. Choosing to grieve rather than suppress it is one significant way you are taking control. Using this guide is another. Every time you choose to work your way through one of the exercises shows you are not helpless. Every self-kindness you do demonstrates you are not helpless.

Take active control over the people you choose to be around, the books you read, and the TV shows you watch. Choose inputs into your life that offer the support you need. For now you can choose to avoid things that bring stress or pressure. This is part of giving yourself the time and space you need to walk your road of grief. This is not feeling sorry for yourself. This is self-preservation.

Be gentle and kind. You are learning a new way to live.

Grief Stew: Garbage Bag of Negative

Get some scraps of paper, larger sticky notes and a small bag you can throw in the garbage. Write your helpless thoughts and feelings on the scraps of paper. Focus on the things that leave you feeling helpless, useless or a failure. When you write out your negativity, visualize letting those feelings drain out on the paper.

For every negative thing you wrote, write an I-am statement on a sticky note that is the opposite. For example, if your negative thing is, "I'm a lousy friend. I don't bother answering emails or texts," the sticky note answer could be, "I am a good friend in the state of suffering. I will tell my friends what I need from them."

Now crumple up the negative scraps of paper and throw them in the garbage bag. Let those helpless feelings become separate from you. Seal the bag, trapping your negative feelings in it and throw it in the garbage.

All the positive sticky notes can go on your bathroom mirror as a reminder of who you really are and how you will express that goodness while suffering in grief.

Reflection: On Purging the Negative

Page 43 in the Honest Grief Notebook

How did it feel to purge the negativity? Was it difficult to be honest and write the negative things? Was it difficult to come up with a positive answer? Why do you think it was this way? Will you use this strategy again when new negative and helpless feelings show up? How did it feel to symbolically get rid of your hopeless feelings and replace them with positive ones? What have you learned from this experience?

Diamond: Book Collection

Did your loved one enjoy reading? If they were a book collector, clear a shelf on your bookcase to display their favourite books. Choose ones they read often, had special meaning, or ones you shared and talked about.

Hopelessness

Death is not a thing we can fix. We can replace a damaged car. We can buy a new pair of jeans when the old ones get a bleach stain. We can replace the batteries in the remote when they wear out. There are many things we can fix, but the loss of a loved one is not one of them. They can't be replaced. Without them, we walk through our days with a big hole in our hearts and an enormous emptiness in our day's activity. You look ahead and there is no expectation of any good ahead. That is hopelessness.

The long days stretch out before you and you wonder, "What's the point?" I felt I was left in a deep, dark valley with nothing to light the way out. I saw no light on the horizon. And for many, many months I lived with a blanketing hopelessness. There was no aspect to my life in which I hadn't faced loss. The loss and the grief were inescapable. My circumstances prevented any relief or restoration from the losses. I just had to live among the ashes of my once happy life for a very long time.

You may find the future seems unrelentingly bleak with no possibility of change. Hopelessness is probably the lowest point of grieving. It can leave you feeling drained of energy and unmotivated. Sinking into a feeling of hopelessness is not wrong. Take each day at a time – deal with it hour by hour, if you have to. Just do your best for that day, that hour, that minute. Your best in that moment is all that is necessary. If that means sitting in your car letting out the deep agony, then give it your best wail. You are walking your journey of grief in your own unique way. Know life will one day give you a spark of hope. In the meantime, it's okay to walk with the companion of hopelessness. Take care of yourself to avoid slipping into clinical depression and thoughts of suicide. If you find yourself thinking these kinds of thoughts, seek professional help immediately.

Be gentle and kind. You are learning a new way to live.

Grief Stew: The Broken Clay Pot

Take a clay pot and break it into larger pieces by dropping it on the driveway or sidewalk, or putting it in a bag and breaking it with a hammer. Use a marker to write on each piece a part of your life that's been affected by the death of your loved one. You don't need to fill them all in right away. It can take time to carefully consider what is broken in your life.

When you are ready you can either piece it back together again or create a broken clay pot garden. (Look up examples of broken pot gardens on the Internet. They are quite lovely.) This could represent putting together the new you – your new way of being.

Reflection: On Brokenness and Restoration

Page 44 in the Honest Grief Notebook

Was it important to put the pieces back together again. Or were you okay with creating something new out of the broken pieces? Why? What have you learned from this experience?

Diamond: Pillow Shirt

Artisans are now making pillows from the shirts of a deceased loved one as a memorial. There are also ones made from a favourite pair of jeans. And there are creative folks who can create a teddy bear or quilt from your loved one's clothing. By keeping some of their clothing in this way, it might make it a bit easier to clear out their closet when you are ready.

Depression

Grief can look a lot like depression. You cry. You have trouble sleeping. You lose your appetite. You don't feel like doing anything. Things you used to love bring you little pleasure. It surprised me every time someone told me I was depressed. In exasperation I'd explain, "I'm not depressed. I'm grieving!"

For me, I still laughed at a good joke and enjoyed a moment of silliness with a friend, although not on my worst days. And while I wanted to die and go to heaven, it wasn't about ending my life, but about wanting to be with my mom again. I had no intention of committing suicide. I just wanted to not go through the rest of my life without her and since she couldn't come back, I wanted to go to heaven. This was not depression. It was simply part of my grief stew.

Expect to feel depressed. Know it's probably not clinical depression. Sadness, loss of appetite and difficulty sleeping are all very normal components of grief – they are common ingredients in grief stew. Expect grief depression to come and go. If you find it staying and becoming the major component of your grief, take a moment and assess if these symptoms are more persistent. Do you have constant and unrelenting feelings of emptiness and despair? Do you rarely or never experience any pleasure or joy? People who have had depression before are more vulnerable to slipping into clinical depression while grieving. If you find your depression symptoms are getting in the way of your day-to-day living, consider connecting with a licensed mental health professional. Some people find a short-term antidepressant takes the edge off and helps restore normal sleep and eating habits. Others find it suppresses their emotions too much and prevents their ability to grieve. But if you are struggling, get professional help.

Be gentle and kind. You are learning a new way to live.

Grief Stew: Inspiration Book

Get some blank cards (or cut heavy stock sheets of letter-sized paper into four). Write out a quote or verse or words of wisdom you found meaningful on each card. Keep on the lookout for fresh things to add to your collection.

You can make your collection into a book by punching two holes on the left side and threading craft string through the holes to tie the cards together. This would allow you to easily add new cards to your book. Or find a box you can keep them in.

When you're feeling low, get a cup of tea and go through your book. Or start your day by reading one of the cards.

Reflection: On What Inspires You

Page 45 in the Honest Grief Notebook

How do you feel when you read through your collection? Consider the content. Do they mostly validate how you are feeling? Or do they mostly give you a vision and hope for your future? Or do you have a mix? What caused you to select the ones you chose to include? What does this say about you and where you are on your grief road? What new areas of focus would you like to add to your collection? What have you learned from these inspirational quotes?

Diamond: Favourite Food Milestone

Think about your loved one's favourite food or drink. Go ahead and indulge in their meal of choice at their favourite restaurant, go to the dairy bar and order their favourite ice cream cone, or visit the bakery and buy some of their favourite fudge brownies. Mark a significant day or anniversary by enjoying their favourite food. Think about the times you enjoyed their favourite food together. Take a selfie of you enjoying their favourite dish.

Despair

Grief certainly has a despondent part. You can come to the place where you wonder, "How can I go on?" You think the pain is too great to survive. Your hopes and dreams are shredded to bits. And you think there's little difference if you lived or died. Feelings of desperation, despondency, pessimism, and loss of hope dance around your mind. You may engage in behaviour that reflects your lack of caring – risky or unhealthy behaviours like riding your motorcycle too fast or drinking too much.

Until you experienced your loss, you probably had no idea the pain would be so unimaginably deep. Onlookers who have not faced this same degree of pain often fail to understand it can be overwhelming and unrelenting. It can feel it's beyond your ability to bear.

Most people are unprepared, even if their loved one died after a long fight with a terminal illness. You can see the black storm approaching on your horizon, but you just can't prepare for the tsunami of grief. In your despair you can't come to grips with their death. You feel agitated and ill, empty yet burdened with a larger-than-you-sized grief, dead inside yet filled with incomprehensible emotions, a sorrow that seems to grow worse every day, and a heart and soul broken beyond repair. All this is normal.

At this deepest, darkest point, you wonder if you'll ever feel joy or contentment again. Addressing your emotions is a formidable task, particularly when living with them seems beyond you. People who are farther along in their journey will tell you it does ease in time. It's not easy. You will never be the same again and it's tough to build your new way of being and find serenity. You are not weird. You are grieving.

It's normal to feel despair in your grief. You are in a deep pit and you're there with what seems like an unrelenting stream of negative emotions as companions in this dark place. Expect to have moments of despair. It's normal to think about your own death, even long to go through death yourself so you can be reunited with your loved one.

If you find yourself actually contemplating suicide or hurting yourself in some way, it's important to tell someone. It's normal to want to be with your loved one. It's dangerous to consider making it happen. If this describes you, connect with a licensed mental health professional.

Be gentle and kind. You are learning a new way to live.

Grief Stew: Postcards from the Abyss

Buy some postcards (or make your own – be sure to follow the guidelines for size of postcards in your country). Send one to yourself each week. Write as though you are a traveller in a foreign land (in a way, you are). Tell what it's like to make your journey through. What have you seen and done in this land? What advice would you give to someone who will travel there? What snippets of wisdom can you share?

Reflection: On Advice from the Abyss

Page 46 in the Honest Grief Notebook

After you have sent and received several cards, what do you think about your advice? Do you have trouble writing the cards? Why or why not? What have you gained from doing this exercise?

Diamond: Video Montage

If you have videos of your loved one, you can make a video montage using short cuts and images to tell their story. If this is not a skill you already possess, there are a number of apps and online sites that make the work fairly easy.

Feeling Overwhelmed

It is not unusual to feel overwhelmed. There is so much pain with grief, and so much devastation to your normal way of life, it can be hard to cope. One major source of this feeling is thinking you have to decide everything immediately. There are some things that need to be handled right away, but focus only on those that are absolutely necessary. Enlist the help of people you trust to help with these decisions. Leave the rest for later.

All life's responsibilities can press in on you leaving you feeling like a steamroller flattened what remained of you. Let go of the things that aren't critical. Let friends and family take on some of your obligations and duties. That way you can focus on the things that are truly necessary – the major one is to do the work of dealing with grief and give yourself a steady diet of self-kindness.

In the depths of grief, it's hard to see the next few steps. It can be impossible to see very far into the future. Trying to figure out things that are impossible to sort out now can lead you to feel it's all too much. You are facing a lot of unknowns. How will you get through this grief? How long will it last? How will you financially survive? How will your life change? When will you feel adequate again? And on and on it goes. Fear can get a strangle hold and flap you around in its gale force winds. Get those thoughts under control.

Release your emotions. If you need to cry, then make it a good one. Find a supportive friend to talk to. Vent your frustration on the pillow. Just find a safe place and let your feelings out. The emotions of grief are not like a fine wine that needs to be bottled and somehow becomes better with age. They really are something you need to address before they get too ripe.

Remember, grief is a process. It is taking one step at a time. Yes, it includes the hard work of dealing with difficult feelings and it includes looking after yourself with small kindnesses. Don't be in a rush to get through it. Accept you are doing your grief in the best way possible. Give yourself the gift of going through your grief in your way and your timing. You are not a victim of your grief. By going through the hard work of addressing your thoughts and feelings, you are in control.

Be gentle and kind. You are learning a new way to live.

Grief Stew: Quit Something

Page 47 in the Honest Grief Notebook

Or quit several things. Everyone has a bucket of I-can-cope juice. Yours is probably nearly dry. And it's going to be awhile before you can take on all the responsibilities you used to manage. List those things you just can't face right now, the things that when you think about them, you feel overwhelmed, and list those things that truly aren't important right now. Beside each item put your decision on whether you are going to let it slide for now, ask someone to help you with it, or turn it over to someone else. If you are going to involve someone else, include their name. Now get in touch with these folks and ask for their help.

Reflection: On Making Space

Page 48 in the Honest Grief Notebook

After several weeks of applying this strategy, have you reduced your feelings of being overwhelmed? Why or why not? Going forward are there any changes you want to make? What do you think about who jumped in and helped? What do you think about those who declined? What have you learned from this experience?

Stress and Pressure

Grief can drain you of your ability to handle life. Things you could normally easily deal with now seem overwhelming. We all have some degree of resiliency – that is the I-can-cope bucket of juice. But grief somehow opened the tap and it all drained out. I often said there's nothing left in my bucket to deal with some new stressor. And you may feel this way too. You might be wondering what happened to that competent, capable person that once was you, but is no more. You are in a season of mourning. It's normal to feel you have all you can handle with your grief. And you have the right to feel that way. You are no wimp.

One of the best things you can do for yourself is to say no to anything that puts you under pressure or you find stressful. Give yourself time to grieve in peace. You need your strength for the hard work of addressing your grief stew. This may mean you need to avoid certain people, places or events. It can also mean letting other's unthinking and unkind words roll off you. For a time it's okay to ensure your environment is the cocoon you need to learn your new way of being. Explain what you need in a nonconfrontational way so you don't hurt others. A good person will listen to what you need and give that to you without judgment.

Be gentle and kind. You are learning a new way to live.

Grief Stew: Oreo Cookie Exercise

Page 49 in the Honest Grief Notebook

Take a few moments to think about what you find stressful or points of pressure. List them in your workbook. (This is the crunchy, brittle part of the cookie.)

Go for a long walk or bike ride. Follow that up with a long soak in the tub with some aromatherapy candles or bath scents. While soaking, think of your favourite beach, mountaintop or whatever place you find peaceful. Visualize yourself taking in the fresh air. Think about the sights, sounds and smells of this place. Spend several minutes immersed in this relaxing environment. Breathe in the peace and blow out your tension. (That's the sugary goodness in the middle of the cookie.)

When you're out of the bath, go back to your list of stressors. Now think about what you will do about each one and list your strategy to deal with your stressors. (This is the other crunchy, brittle part of the cookie.)

Tips for Coping with Stress

Avoid things that overwhelm (See Feeling Overwhelmed):
- It's okay to say no and draw boundaries
- Avoid people who cause stress or create problems for you
- Get rid of unnecessary responsibilities and tasks
- Don't try to control things that are out of your control
- Manage your anxiety
- Keep your to-do lists realistic and manageable
- Ask for and accept help

Deal with your anger, resentment, regret, self-reproach and remorse:
- Express your feelings
- Address feelings keeping you stuck like anger, frustration, guilt, regret, remorse, etc

Look after yourself:
- Practise self-kindnesses
- Laugh easily
- Eat healthy
- Exercise
- Get enough sleep
- Seek support, talk with people who won't judge

- Reduce substance use
- Take things one day at a time
- Spend time with animals
- Be intentional about establishing some quiet time
- Treat yourself as you would a suffering friend
- Acknowledge the progress you make every day, even if it's as simple as getting out of bed
- Be vigilant to keep problems in perspective

Reflection: On the Oreo Cookie

Page 50 in the Honest Grief Notebook

Consider the progress you have made in dealing with the emotions of grief. How successfully have you dealt with the stress? If there are areas where you have been less successful, what can you do to improve things? What are the reasons for your success in the areas you are coping with? How do you think the exercise and relaxation affected your creativity in finding solutions to your stress? What have you learned from this experience?

Diamond: Playlist of Songs

Create a playlist of your loved one's favourite songs. Play the music anytime you want to bring them a little closer in memory. If they used a smart phone, you can figure out their favourite songs by the number of times a song was played. Also check if they rated the music. You can use the four- and five-star songs.

Re-Entry Troubles

Anguish and sorrow are not the end of your story. Grief stew is a chapter in your life, perhaps a weighty chapter, but a chapter nonetheless. Every chapter ends and you begin a new one. Just as one chapter does not define a book, so your life will not be defined by your loss or losses, but by the new way of being you build. Your new life will not be better or worse than your old life, just different. You will find serenity in this new way of being and you will enjoy life again.

As you re-enter normal life, you will have familiar patterns of living, marriage and friendships that will bring comfort, but be open to trying a new way of living. Your family structure may have changed, your priorities may have shifted and you may choose new friends, a new job, new city or a new cause. Have patience as you try restoring your old ways. Some may not fit anymore. You will explore a variety of new ways. Not everything you try will be something you wish to keep. All of this restoration and exploration can seem disruptive. Remember, change is a learning opportunity. Take the opportunity to find and form the most comfortable way of being.

Be patient with the process. When a huge speedboat screams by your little kayak the waves threaten to swamp, but in time they come farther apart and less intense until finally they settle into gentle laps. Instead of grief that rages as mountainous waves that threaten to drown, your grief will quiet down to a gentle ebb and flow that brings tranquility and whose sound is a pleasant reminder of life.

Don't resist putting down your new roots along with your old ones. In time your life will bear fruit again.

Be gentle and kind. You are learning a new way to live.

Grief Stew: Before I Die

Page 51 in the Honest Grief Notebook

Yes, this is something like a bucket list. Where a bucket list tends to be adventurous and unique things to do, like walk the Great Wall of China, or visit the Taj Mahal at midnight, this list is meant to include those big things as well as other more everyday things too.

Think about new hobbies, different activities, local and distant adventures, nearby and global places to go, people you want to spend time with, things you want to do (like what rooms you will redecorate), things you want to change. Think about all the things you will do with your life ahead and list them.

Don't shy away from adventures. Whether it is overseas (like sleep in a Mongolian yurt, ride a reindeer in Siberia, stay in an ice hotel in Norway), or it is close to home (like wall climbing, zip lining, sky diving or scuba diving), it's okay to make a fresh start and explore a part of you you haven't yet explored. Think about what you'd love to do.

Let yourself dream big, then follow your heart. It has successfully led you through the storms of grief. Let it lead you into new dreams. Take some risks.

Reflection: On Before I Die

Page 52 in the Honest Grief Notebook

What is the value of this list? How do you feel looking over your list? Is it important to do everything on it? Why or why not? What have you learned about yourself – your hopes and dreams?

Diamond: Old Photos Renewed

Take an old photo (or several) that has meaning for you and your loved one. It could be of the two of you at your first house, your child in front of the school on the first day, or the café where you took a picture of you together. Return to that place and take a second picture of you there, remembering those special moments again. Those memories are not erased. They are renewed with your visit to those places and your capturing new moments with new photos. You can print both the old and new photos, and add them to your notebook or a scrapbook.

New Friends

There are a number of people who knew your loved one and know of your loss. Some either don't know what to do, or do the wrong things, or simply just avoid you. I've heard them called step-back friends. These are the folks who are unsupportive or even toxic, and either you or they stepped back from your relationship. They just can't deal with your grief and act like it might be contagious. Or you find you can't afford to listen to their toxic judgments. I had one person I chose to step back from because I couldn't handle all the judgments. She proclaimed I had built up a wall and was keeping everybody out. Because she couldn't imagine I would be getting support from anyone but her, she dumped another judgment on me.

Once they step back from you, you'll rarely hear from them again. While you're glad to be free of their destructive words, it still hurts to lose people you thought would have your back. It's not like grief isn't hard enough. You face losing friends at the time you need them most.

For those you need to step away from, it's hard to do so without hurting them.

On the other side, there are the step-forward friends – those true blue friends that stand with you. They are the ones you count on to be there. They accept your grief, and the length and depth of your grief road. They are the ones you can lean on. They love you without putting conditions on their love. They show their thoughtfulness in many small ways that hold great meaning for you.

Then there are all the people you've met since your loved one's death, and all those you will meet in your future who didn't know them, and will never know the person you were before the death. It can be quite difficult navigating a new relationship. New relationships can be so fragile when first forming. So when is it a good time to let them know you just spent a year watching the life drain out of your loved one? When should you tell about the horrific accident that suddenly ripped them out of your life? When is a good time to tell about their suicide? When should you tell about the devastating loss of a child? You feel you want to protect this un-tainted new friendship, but you also need to be honest about who you are.

One blogger wrote a post, *When to Drop the "Dead Baby" Bomb*. She wonders what to say about the death of her baby and when to say it. It can be difficult and there's a temptation to say nothing and simply enjoy the new friendship without introducing a dead spouse bomb, a dead parent bomb, a dead child bomb, a dead sibling bomb, or a dead whatever bomb. At some point conversation will give you the opportunity to tell of your loss. Think about how much you want to tell, and how you would like the conversation to go. Do you want to really talk about it? Do you want to share a story? Or do you want to make a brief statement and say no more? In the same way your loss and grief shone a light on those friends who truly accept and care for you without judgment, so too will your explanation shine a light on those new friends who enjoy this new you and care without it.

When you are ready, when your friendship is ready, you have great memories to share with others. Telling your new friends stories about who your loved one was means they get to meet this person that still holds a big part of your heart.

Be gentle and kind. You are learning a new way to live.

Grief Stew: Star Lights in the Long Night

Page 53 in the Honest Grief Notebook

In the dark depths of grief, there are sparks of light that shine through and onto you – things like the soup a friend brought by, or the card someone sent with a photo, or a good story someone shared about your loved one. Take a moment with your cup of tea to make note of these. In your numbness and fog, you may lose track of these over time if you don't write them down. Include the name of the star in your life, the date, a description of what they did and what it meant to you.

Reflection: On the Value of Friends

Page 54 in the Honest Grief Notebook

Consider the length of your list, the number of people who have brought a bit of light into your darkness, and the meaning of what they have done. Is it filled mostly with step-forward friends or are there some new ones in there too? What impact has this had on your life? What do you feel about giving back?

Diamond: Dinner Date

Page 55 in the Honest Grief Notebook

Make a dinner date with someone who knew your loved one. Share your interesting, funny and poignant stories, and listen to theirs. You might hear of events you didn't know about. You may want to write down the details (at the table or afterward).

Consider making dinner dates with a number of your loved one's friends, collecting their stories each time.

New Strengths

You don't know how strong you are until strong is the only choice. Most people who have gone through deep grief say that from doing the hard work of dealing with grief stew, and from putting one foot in front of the other and just surviving, new strengths surface you didn't know you had. Developing new strengths is probably the last thing you have in mind, but in learning to live a new way, in learning to live with a great big hole in your heart, new strengths just naturally develop. And there's nothing wrong with celebrating an emerging strength.

By the time you're reading this section, you've probably been on the grief road for some time. You've probably experienced most of the negative emotions of grief – many times over. The fact you've survived the most difficult time in your life tells of a new strength. You got up in the morning. You showered. You shopped for groceries. You ate. You walked outside. You fed the kids. You did the laundry. You wept. You are working through your grief. You survived. These are all strengths you couldn't fathom early on.

You will discover more strength as your new way of being emerges. You might find it difficult to acknowledge a new strength because you've staked out this place to grieve and worry that admitting you have strength may somehow end your grief work prematurely. Echoes of, "It's time you snap out of it," haunt your thoughts. You fear onlookers are going to spot your new strength and tell you it's time to move on. Remember, this is your grief and your road to travel. Only you know when you have all the strength and resources to walk through the rest of your life. Only you know when your I-can-cope juice bucket has enough in it to embrace life again.

Finding your new way of being is a bit like going to school. When you've learned to add two and two, there is still much to learn to complete the grade. Accept you are learning and growing. And celebrate your new strengths. It doesn't take away from the difficulty of your grief road at all.

Be gentle and kind. You are learning a new way to live.

Grief Stew: One Word

Page 56 in the Honest Grief Notebook

There's a book called *My One Word* by Mike Ashcraft and Rachel Olsen. It is an idea to replace New Year's resolutions that typically fail. These broken resolutions are replaced with a single word that acts as a point of clarity and focus. It's like a point on the horizon where you point your ship. Then when the year is done, you can measure your progress toward that one word – how far did your ship travel?

You are now embarking on a life with a new way of being. You've dealt with the stormy emotions of grief and are finding the serene way you will live with a hole in your heart, and a missing loved one in your life. This is the perfect time to pick a word as a point to steer your ship.

List all the words that describe that serene person you wish to be. Choose words that go deep into your heart, your soul, your character – words like peace, stability, connected, balanced, joyful, unafraid or focused.

Now choose one that sums up who you want to be or how you want to live over the next year. This will be the direction where you move your life. It is the compass you will use when making decisions. It will lead your steps. You will see your world through the new lens of this word. Circle that word. (Note: One Word 365 is a global community of people using this strategy. You can join with others on the same journey.)

Reflection: On the Power of One Word

Page 56 in the Honest Grief Notebook

Every quarter reflect on your progress. What impact has this word had on your life? Did you join a group online? If so, what impact did that have on your engagement? What have you learned from the One Word commitment?

Diamond: One Distinction

Page 56 in the Honest Grief Notebook

Much like the One Word you chose for yourself, this is the One Word of Distinction for your loved one. Take some time to write out all their great characteristics. Think about their individuality and integrity. In looking through your list of words and thinking about what you loved most, choose one word that distinguishes and sets them apart. This will be their One Distinction.

New Patterns

Part of the purpose of this guide is to help you develop and identify new patterns. A gigantic boulder of loss crashed into your life, flattened your world, disrupted your stable reality and plunged you into grief. Loss forces you into new patterns of existence. You have a choice of remaining stuck in the patterns of loss, or you can determine to do the work of addressing your grief and establishing new patterns of your own choosing, not those forced on you. By working through your grief stew, you will be laying the foundation for your new way of being. You have the opportunity of being intentional in what patterns you bring into your life. This is your chance to sort through the patterns and throw away those that no longer serve a good purpose, and select those that will support your new way of being.

You may find your life's purpose has shifted, what you value has changed and your goals are different. It can take time for these new patterns to emerge. That's a part of what comes from dealing with your grief stew. It's quite normal to discover what you thought was important is no longer of value, what you chose as entertainment is no longer satisfying, even people you thought were fun are no longer aligned to you and your new direction. It's okay to shed old values and goals with the old you who was shattered by loss. The old you just doesn't exist anymore. It was destroyed. You can cling to that crippled and damaged you, or you can do your grief stew work and embrace the changes that come from it.

Don't try to rush through this process. It takes time to pick up the pieces of your broken life and build something new. It comes one step at a time. Take your time and be purposeful in your decisions. And as always, look after yourself.

Be gentle and kind. You are learning a new way to live.

Grief Stew: Who Am I Now?

Page 57 in the Honest Grief Notebook

Values are defined as a person's principles or standards of behaviour – your judgment of what is important in life. What do you value in life? Think about words that describe how you are or would like to be with others, your finances, relationships and roles, the present and future, priorities, faith and spirituality, social life, physical and emotional health.

Now select from the list approximately ten values. List them in order of importance to you. Beside each word write a number from one to ten to indicate how fully you are living that value right now (one not at all, ten fully).

Reflection: On New Values and Patterns

Page 57 in the Honest Grief Notebook

What things can you do to more fully live your values? What thoughts came up while you did this exercise? Consider your values in deciding your life's purpose and vision for the future. Has anything changed from who you were before your loved one died? What goals would you like to now pursue? What new patterns have emerged from doing grief stew work? What have you learned from the grief experience?

Diamond: Wear Your Love

Find a piece of jewellery or an item of clothing from your loved one to wear. It's a way of letting people know how important they were to you and to help you still feel connected. People often choose a ring, a watch, a sweater or coat. Choose something that was uniquely associated with your loved one and brings you fond memories.

Ruminating

Pondering, meditating, musing, remembering and reflecting are all part of grief. Ruminating is when you become caught in an endless loop, going through a thought over and over again. In grief there can be a benefit to short-term rumination. It can push you toward exploring why something happened. The act of recognizing and exploring to come to an understanding is a component of dealing with your grief stew. Many aspects of loss are real and do require a well-thought-out decision such as changed financial circumstances. The challenge in grief is you may not initially have the mental focus to sort out what to do and these thoughts can exist as rumination for a short time.

If it becomes a chronic thought and you can't find your way out of the loop, you can become stuck in pain, or worse, find yourself swirling downward into a very dark place that will need a licensed mental health professional to help you find your path out.

There are a few strategies various people have found helpful. When the looping thoughts begin, try a pleasant and distracting thought or activity like one of the self-kindnesses. Immerse yourself in it, fully attending the sights, sounds, smells, tastes and feels.

Focus on the rational truth, not your looping thoughts. Challenge the validity of what you are thinking. Put things into context (the conditions) and focus on a positive perspective (the explanation). For example, if you are struggling with ruminating thoughts of something you failed to do, remember the positive things you did for your loved one. Remember the happy times together. Recall all you did right.

Admit rumination will lead nowhere good. Deliberately let go of the negative. Replace the destructive thoughts with a positive commitment. When the rumination starts, stop it in its tracks by stating your commitment that starts with, "From now on I want to..."

Don't try to deal with everything immediately. And don't give up. You can't bring your loved one back. You can't change the fact of loss. But you have control over what you do and think today and tomorrow. Focus on the things you can control.

Avoid judging yourself. Be gentle and kind. You are learning a new way to live.

Grief Stew: New Ticker Tape

Page 58 in the Honest Grief Notebook

You know that scrolling text that appears on the bottom of the screen of the news channel? It's called a ticker tape. It just keeps repeating the same stories over and over again. This is much like what's happening when you ruminate. What is your looping story?

Now challenge the validity of that story. What were the circumstances? Consider what you knew at the time and what choices you had. What is a rational explanation? Think about why it happened that way. How would someone else explain it? Can you now see an alternate way of viewing it? If so, you're ready to write a new statement for your ticker tape. This statement is focused on the positive light in which you chose to think about the situation. For example, if you are ruminating about that thing you failed to do, you could answer these thoughts with, "From now on I want to deal with my regrets right away. I remember all the good I did." Write your new ticker tape statement. Whenever you begin ruminating repeat it to yourself.

Reflection: On Controlling Destructive Thoughts

Page 59 in the Honest Grief Notebook

What were the challenges in letting go of that negative looping thought? What were the circumstances in which you were most effective at stopping the destructive ruminations? What have you learned from this experience with controlling ruminations?

Diamond: Loved Letters

Did your loved one write letters? Do you have some of their correspondence? When you go through their writings, collect your favourites and organize them in a special display container. Make and decorate an envelope booklet (check out instructions here https://www.marthastewart.com/270217/envelope-books-cloth-binding-how-to) or buy one already made on Etsy.

Remembering

You are having a good day. Then out of the blue something hits you, and the wave of pain and sadness wash over you. It might be a song, a flash of memory as you're chatting with someone, a child walking home from school, the sound of a lawnmower, the smell of toast and coffee, or a million other things. And that triggers the flood of love that swirls in your heart with no place to go

Remembering is an important part of loving someone. Don't stop remembering. It is in your memories that you can continue to fully express your love. It's okay to weep over your photo album – to touch the images and remember the good times. It's okay to sob over their empty coffee mug and remember all the lazy Saturday mornings. It's okay to drown the teddy bear in tears as you remember the smell of the bath on their skin and tininess of their body as you tucked them in at night. Really, it's okay to remember with emotion. You are still raw from the loss. You are grieving, and if you're honest, it feels good to pour out your heart. While it hurts, it feels good to remember. Those memories are treasures to hang onto.

In time, you will find you can tell a story of your loved one without falling apart. You can look at a picture, watch a video, hold the teddy bear and remember without the devastating sorrow. Sure, you might feel sad, but you are no longer falling apart. Your new way of being is coming to a place of serenity with the hole in your heart and the missing person in your life. Know this place of serenity doesn't mean an absence of sadness. One definition of serenity is that you are marked by quietude – which means calm and free of storms. The tumult of emotions, like anguish and sorrow when the loss is still a raw, gaping wound within, will subside. But sadness is not a stormy emotion. Even in serenity, it's perfectly normal to have moments of sadness along with moments of laughter and dreaming and being.

Let remembering be a regular part of your life. Each memory is a gemstone worthy of you rolling it around and exploring the details of its beauty. Hold those memories up to the light and watch how they shine.

Be gentle and kind. You are learning a new way to live.

Grief Stew and Diamond: Capture the Fireflies

Have you noticed how fleeting your memory is? You remember a story and it lights up your brain, but the next day you can't remember it at all. It's like the light of a firefly – a transient beauty. Keep a little notebook with you and capture these memories as you think of them.

Reflection: On Capturing Fireflies

Page 60 in the Honest Grief Notebook

Remembering can bring your pain of loss to the forefront, but how is this experience helpful? What will you do with the "fireflies" you captured in your notebook? What have you learned from this experience?

Share and Talk

There are two categories of stories in grief. One is your unique story of loss and grief stew, which includes the death of your loved one, your pain and suffering. Then there are the stories of life with your loved one, which includes your relationship, the good times, the funny times, all those unforgettable memories and stories.

At first, your grief stew story will require more time and more telling – even retelling. This is how you fathom the loss and absorb the irreversible change in your life. This retelling is an important part of coming to grips with your mental anguish. Find a few supportive friends who will listen without judgment and are okay with the pain of sorrow without trying to stop it, and just pour your heart out.

But it is the stories of life with your loved one that will bring meaning to your grief, and ensure you are able to bring your love for that person forward with you into the rest of your life. While you need time to yourself to work through the painful parts, you will want time to swap memories with others who knew your loved one. You may want to become a collector of their stories.

Remember, both stories (of your loved one and your grief) are an important part to finding your way of integrating this loss into your new way of being.

Be gentle and kind. You are learning a new way to live.

Grief Stew: Life Inventory Part 2

Page 61 in the Honest Grief Notebook

Take stock, again. Review what you listed in part 1 of this exercise (in the Denial and Disbelief section, pg. 25 in this book and pg. 6 in the Honest Grief Notebook). Now list what you've gained – those positive things that have come into your life since you've worked on your grief stew. It could be people and friendships, personal strengths, new hope, your vision for your future, or rituals and practices that have brought meaning. Come back often and add items as you think of them.

Reflection: On Grief Stew Gains

Page 62 in the Honest Grief Notebook

How did you feel when you reviewed the list of things lost and maintained? How did it feel to create your list of things gained? Did you find this exercise easy or difficult and why? What does all you've gained say about you? What did you learn from this experience?

Diamond: Life Story

Organize a story potluck with friends and family of your loved one. Have everyone bring recipe cards each with a story they want to share that includes your loved one. Be sure they date the story with at least the year and the month, if they can remember. Have each share their stories in chronological order. Collect all the recipe cards at the end.

You can create a timeline of your loved one's life from all the stories on an accordion-style paper book. (check out how to make the book here http://www.readbrightly.com/diy-accordion-book/)

Finding Courage

Courage is said to be quiet, steady and unfailing strength to persevere. It's the bridge between fear and action. When living with loss it takes courage to willingly walk through the darkness, turmoil, and solitude to serenity at the other side. Walking through this black valley is the only way you will find a place where you can enjoy the memories of your loved one without chaotic emotions. You may not see the light at the other end for quite some time, but continue to forge your way through the valley. Grief is messy business. It's not convenient. It's hard. But the only way to help these difficult feelings pass is to get in and muck through them. It is the only way to wholeness. It takes courage to face the hurricane of grief.

Our society will press you to move on. Even onlookers find it uncomfortable and don't want the bedlam of grief to encroach on their lives. You may find to forge your path through grief means you have to go against others' expectations. And that takes courage as well.

Because of your courage to walk through the storms of grief, you will find a way of living in peace with the hole in your heart and the chasm in your tomorrows. You will be integrating your love and memories into a life of serenity.

What does it take to have the courage to walk through all that is grief stew? It takes a daily persistence to deal with it and to sugar your days with plenty of kindnesses. Every morning you commit to taking another step. You get up and press on. You invest the thinking time you need to work through the grief stew exercises. You apply what you learn. You are patient with your heart and mind as you find your way. Courage is continuing your journey despite the judgments and shaming by others. You confront the overwhelming pain of loss and extreme emotion. You endure the uncertainty of when it will all end with a determination to find your way.

Did you know many people give up on dealing with grief stew? They get knocked down one too many times by the challenging emotions and finally decide to not get up anymore. You are still standing. You have courage within you. You haven't given up – you are courageous. You keep seeking good friends, the step-forward friends despite the many that tear you down with words – you are courageous. You could say you don't have a choice, but you do. You could have given up, but you didn't – you are courageous. You are navigating your way through this mess without a map – you are courageous.

If you are looking for your courage, it's already inside you. You have the heart of a lion.

Be gentle and kind. You are learning a new way to live.

Grief Stew: Courage Jar

How about a little courage in a jar? Get a mason jar with a lid. Write short affirmations of the good actions you take that build your courage to continue your journey to your new way of being. You can hand write the affirmations on strips of colourful pieces of paper, and then put them in the jar. Add a label that says, "Courage in a jar. Read one every day."

Reflection: On a Courage Jar

Page 63 in the Honest Grief Notebook

What was the most challenging part of writing your own courage jar affirmations? What has the impact of writing and reading your affirmations been on your courage to face tomorrow? What have you learned from this experience?

Diamond: Wisdom Jar

Create a second jar that contains the wisdom of your loved one. You can also include funny or humorous sayings. When your collections are a significant size, consider creating a strength jar that contains a mix of your courage and your loved one's wisdom affirmations. Share your combined wisdom with someone struggling with grief and loss.

Faith

The brother of Dr. Larry Crabb died in a plane crash. Seven years later Larry, a Christian psychologist, was still grieving. It angered him when someone said to him it's been seven years and he should get a grip. He's very clear about the length and depth of grief, and the role of faith in the midst of it. He says knowing the Lord and receiving His comfort does not take away the ache of loss. In fact, he says he will continue to ache until he's reunited with his brother in heaven.

Don't expect your faith to eliminate the pain of grief. When you love and the object of your love dies, there is unrelenting pain. Initially tumultuous emotions threaten to drown us. Words of faith meant to comfort can be quickly blown away by the howling gales of sorrow. Don't question your faith if you don't find a future promise of reunion very comforting today. This day you are without your loved one. Let yourself grieve your loss. The goal isn't getting rid of the pain. No, the pain of grief will be with you for the remainder of your life. The goal is finding a way to live with it and yet not be controlled by it. The goal is to do the work you need to do to calm the storms.

So if we must live with the pain, what is the role of faith? Some people find faith brings a comfort through their pain, not instead of it. When a loved one dies, you walk through the valley of the shadow of death. If faith was a part of your life, continue to express it in the ways that seem appropriate to you. Choose to be with people who support your religious beliefs. Know that feeling angry with God for your loss is quite normal. Find a friend who will accept your feelings of loss and abandonment without judging your faith. Remember, having a faith doesn't insulate you from times of tribulation, nor does it protect you from needing to talk through your thoughts and feelings. Feel free to express your faith and your grief.

Some grieving people can't hear the comfort in their religion until the chaos of grief fades. Some find their journey along the grief road draws them closer to their faith. Others turn away from it in anger, or set out on a quest of finding an alternative spiritual place of comfort. All these responses are quite normal.

If your faith brings you comfort in the storm, lean into it. If not, know you will address your faith when the time is right. For me, I still believed in God, but I watched a steady stream of losses come into my life. No aspect of my life was left untouched by profound loss. I wondered when the loss brigade would be finished dumping more grief on my life. I came to the place where I told God I stopped believing goodness would return in my life. I looked at the trend line of two to three years and if it continued, I could expect nothing but more loss. Mine was not a crisis in faith, but a crisis in hope. I've heard it takes strength and honesty to raise your fists full of bitterness to the God of love. I did, and I can tell you I did return to a place of hope again.

It takes a strong faith to pursue God after such deeply troubling questions. It's okay with God if you come to Him with these difficult thoughts. It is not a faith crisis. As with the rest of the grief stew, work through your thoughts of faith as you can.

If you're not a person of faith, don't be afraid to explore your spirituality. In the midst of grief stew, inspirational reading, prayer, meditation, and community worship can bring a sense of belonging, comfort and direction as you cope with your loss. You can deepen and strengthen your spiritual life. Seek those things that work best for you – whether it is prayer, song, worship, meditation or reading Scripture. Ask God questions, and then allow yourself to be open to the inner guidance you receive. Listen to the whispers of your heart and soul.

Be gentle and kind. You are learning a new way to live.

Grief Stew: Wisdom of the Aged

Connect with an older person (grandparent, older aunt or uncle, or if you have no older folks in your family, seek out an older person from your church or community). Ask them to tell you about their most cherished memories. Ask them if they would handle things differently. Listen as they talk of their past, and times when they were full of life and hope. Listen for moments when they felt fear or sadness. Ask about when they struggled and how they handled it. Would they do anything differently?

Reflection: Wisdom of the Aged

Page 64 in the Honest Grief Notebook

What did you find remarkable or surprising in what they told you? What is one sentence that really stuck with you and carried meaning? What are your biggest takeaways from this experience? Someday you may be that older wise person sharing your hopes, dreams and struggles with another generation. Keep what you are learning from this experience in your heart so you can share what is most meaningful.

Hope

Just as courage is the bridge from fear to action, grief is the bridge from devastating loss to living a fulfilling life again. In that sense, there is hope in grief knowing the tough work of addressing all your thoughts and emotions will bring you to a place of living with the loss without the chaos of emotion – finding your new way of being.

In the height of the grief storm, when mountainous waves of anguish threaten to drown you and hurricane winds of sorrow suck out your very breath, it's hard to see anything on the horizon, let alone anything worth setting your hopes on. Yes, there will be days when you feel there is no hope in your life. And you may live without hope for a lot longer than just a few days.

My circumstances were such that a health complication made it impossible to work. While struggling with my health and other significant losses, the loss parade continued to bring more. I gave up hoping there would be an end. I tired of trying to get back on my feet again and again only to be knocked down by another loss. I looked hard into the horizon, yet I saw no relief that would lift me out of the destroyed remains of my shattered life. And I saw no end to the time I would have to spend surrounded by loss. I had two to three years of losses, and spent a year without hope. I know it is hard. In fact, most days felt impossible. I often said, "I can't handle any more."

If you too find yourself without hope, know you can survive. You can put one foot in front of the other and gradually make your way through the valley of grief. Treat yourself to extra self-kindnesses. Look to do something good each day, even a little thing. Know one day something will enter your pathway – a new job, a supportive friend, an afternoon without the tsunami of pain, a temporary lightening of the burden because of a funny movie or a little joy as you laugh at your pet's antics. These are all proof you will find a new way of being, that this grief stew really is a bridge to life.

Consider this. You could have chosen to suppress your thoughts and emotions, and muddle through the rest of your life with that loss-crippled, damaged you but you didn't. You actually chose hope when you chose to grieve because you are intentionally and deliberately moving toward your new way of being. In time, more significant hope will return. It is part of the serenity you will find.

Be gentle and kind. You are learning a new way to live.

Grief Stew: Teleport to Your Future

Page 65 in the Honest Grief Notebook

You know those science fiction shows where they teleport all over the universe? They even teleport into the future. Imagine you could take a look at who you will be three to five years from now. Imagine you have discovered your new way of being and found serenity in your loss. Who are you in this future? What are you doing? Where are you living? Who are your friends and what do you do with them? What does your life look like?

Take some time to dream about this future. Write down all the significant things you visualize.

Reflection: On Your Future

Page 66 in the Honest Grief Notebook

How hard was it to think about yourself in the future? How different is your new way of being from your old life? How different is it from your current life? What would it take to get there? What have you learned from this experience?

Diamond: Name a Star

Did you know you can have a star named after your loved one? There are a number of organizations that will select a star and add your loved one's name to their databases. They will send you documentation related to this star. (Here is one example https://www.nameastarlive.com). Some even take your loved one's name on a document and release it into orbit.

Officially stars are numbers, not names. While there are common names for certain stars, like the North Star or Regulus, these names are not official as they differ in various languages and cultures. So when you have a star named after your loved one, it is not official. However it's neat to think of your loved one's name circling the earth even if it isn't official.

Gratitude

We now live in a world where gratitude is a buzzword. I'm sure you've seen the hashtags. You've heard someone who ends a horrible story with, "But I should be grateful. It's not like I have cancer." Well, what if you just watched your loved one die of cancer? Are you obligated to feel gratitude? Should you be saying, "At least I'm still alive?" What if you would rather slip through death's door and be with your loved one?

When life is incredibly unfair, and deals you a painful loss or a whole pile of them, is it okay to just want to sit in the sadness just for a little while? Does that make you a totally ungrateful person? Or just an honest one? Does sitting on the ash heap of your life, weeping over your losses, suddenly change your core character to unthankful?

I'm not advocating you wallow in self-pity and become stuck there. I am suggesting it's a normal response to feel cheated by death. If you are a Christian, then you already believe humans weren't created with death as a part of life. So is it wrong to acknowledge you feel ripped off because death claimed the life of your loved one? Make no excuses for the dark and bitter place where you find yourself. Read about Naomi in the Bible – she told people just to call her bitter instead of Naomi. But it didn't last forever. Nor will yours. She eventually stood up from the ashes of her life, and found a new life and new blessings that restored her gratitude.

In time you will rise up off your ash heap too. You will be able to honestly look at your life and see things you are genuinely grateful for. Both your anger at the injustice of your loss and regaining your ability to be grateful are part of the grief stew. Both are normal.

When ready, you can start recording things you are grateful for. Committing to putting your gratitude on paper can shift your focus from the horrible events you have endured – and the pain you are in – to something positive. You are intentionally opening your heart to the new you. You are finding your way from the chaos of grief to the serenity of it.

The bottom line is this. Don't feel ashamed because you feel the injustice of death. It isn't a crisis of character. It's just accepting your authentic feelings and letting them out. Remember, grief stew is a complex mix of emotions that need to be let out and addressed. In grief pessimism often shows up before gratitude. And that's okay. For me, every time a new loss hit while still struggling with the last one, I'd be thrown right back to the beginning of the grief road, only with a bigger set of emotions to deal with and more grisly bits of stew. If I can find my way through, so can you.

Be gentle and kind. You are learning a new way to live.

Grief Stew: Objects Are Closer than They Appear

Page 67 in the Honest Grief Notebook

Gratitude may seem a long way off and it can seem that way for a long time. You may be surprised it is actually closer than it appears. This may be difficult at first, but regularly take time to add to a gratitude book. You can buy a small notebook, or use cards to write on, or cut some paper into quarters. Write short statements of why you are grateful today. Start with I or My and write in the present tense (I am grateful today...)

There are a lot of gratitude statements you can find online, but try to write your own. Here are some questions to help you think about the good that has come into your life.

What rituals, practices, exercises, activities, locations, or people have helped you feel peace, love, joy, meaning, belonging, inclusion, strong, or any other positive feeling?

In looking through your reflections throughout this book, what are some of the lessons you've learned or ways you've grown? Can you see gratitude in those reflections?

What are some of the ways you see working through your grief stew as influencing your life and your future?

If you used cards, feel free to decorate the other side with doodles, sketches, wrapping paper, or whatever you wish. You may want to keep your cards in a box or tied with a ribbon to mark them as special. On a day when you're feeling low, look through them. And don't forget to keep adding to your collection.

Reflection: On Finding Your Gratitude

Page 68 in the Honest Grief Notebook

What, if anything, made this a difficult task? How has this activity focused you on the positive aspects of your life? What have you learned from reviewing all your reflections?

Diamond: Make a Donation

Did your loved one support a particular charity? Is there a charity associated with their cause of death? Find a reputable one and give a donation in their name. It's a way of aligning with those things they valued or of helping to prevent the needless death of others.

132

Serenity, Not Closure or Acceptance

Can you actually accept the loss? Is there closure to grief? Acceptance and closure are words that seem impossible, yet are a standard part of the language of psychology. The hole in your heart and chasm in your life will be with you all your remaining days. So the word closure just doesn't apply. It means there is an end. Short of your loved one returning from the dead, there will be no end, no closure.

Acceptance is another word you may find difficult to embrace. The death of your loved one will never be acceptable. Your grief road will lead you to your new way of being, of finding a place of peace with the new shape of your heart and soul, of looking to your future in serenity. You'll have eaten a lot of grief stew to get to this place of integration or reconciliation. But at no point will you have found your loss acceptable.

You'll have learned to face your grief storm, to embrace the pain, to let your sorrow take centre stage for awhile and let the tumult of emotions wash over you. You'll have discovered by releasing them in your life for a time they rage for awhile, diminish and then lose their grip on you. For a long time you thought you would drown, but you've finally found firm footing and are walking toward the shore, with the gentle waves lapping at your legs.

Part of you has died. It will never come back. By the time you get to shore you'll have changed. In building your new you, there are new parts born out of the work you've done with your grief stew.

If you're not there just yet, let the voices of those who have been through their own grief speak hope into your journey. While grief is universal, you are a unique person forging your own way to the unique, new you. There is no right or wrong way through. For now be grateful anytime your feet find a sandbar in the midst of your storm. And don't be pushed into finding closure to something that will never close, or accepting the unacceptable. You will find serenity in the new you.

Be gentle and kind. You are learning a new way to live.

Grief Stew: Sandy Toes

Pages 69 and 70 in the Honest Grief Notebook

As serenity begins to re-enter your life, take a moment to write about these times. It's important to mark when your feet land on solid ground, even for a short time. It's evidence your life will not be filled with the storms of grief forever. Include details of people, place and time. Every time you add a new entry, take a moment to read through your other ones.

Reflection: On the Goodness of a Sandbar

Page 71 in the Honest Grief Notebook

How did the first signs of serenity feel? Once you started experiencing it, how quickly did more moments come into your life? What have you learned from these serenity moments?

Diamond: Name a Rose or Fund a Plaque

You can have a rose named after your loved one with the folks who create new cultivars. It's quite expensive, but a unique way of remembering your loved one. Since most would find this unaffordable, you can arrange with your local city or town to put a plaque on a park bench. Go sit on that bench often!

Letting Go

We can hang onto things trying to hold onto the person who died or the thing we lost. It may be clothing, possessions, memories, photos, rooms, plants, furniture, letters – things they loved. There will be people that tell you to let go and move on. Trust yourself. You will know when you are ready to let go and say goodbye. There may be things you will never let go of, and that's okay.

Give yourself as much time and space to hold on – stare at the photos, visit that favoured place, sleep with the shirt. There may come a day when you know you don't need to cling to that thing any longer. Just don't let anyone pressure or guilt you into saying goodbye before you are ready.

And when you are, you will remember with fondness the sweet farewell. And you can accept the release of that thing that helped you through the dark days.

Be gentle and kind. You are learning a new way to live.

Grief Stew: Sky Lantern Release

Light a sky lantern with your loved one's name on it. Add a message and release it at night. If you have lost several family members, you could release a number of lanterns at once. They can be bought online from Amazon. (Check if you need a permit to release a sky lantern, and do not release the lantern where it is a potential fire hazard.) If a sky lantern is not a possibility, there are biodegradable water lanterns that can be floated on the lake or pool, or you could release biodegradable balloons into the sky.

Reflection: On a Sweet Release

Page 72 in the Honest Grief Notebook

How did it feel to release the lanterns or balloons? How did others feel about it? What did you learn from this experience? What do you value from it?

Diamond: Shadow Box Keepsake

Collect items of your loved one that represent them – their glasses, photos, jewellery, watch, pipe, flowers from the funeral, flag, page from their favourite book, favourite poem, fishing lures, favourite shirt as the background, things they wrote, key fob, teddy bear, baby booties, etc. Buy a shadow box and assemble these things into a memorial artwork.

Handling Special Days

There can be many days over the course of a year you find difficult – Valentine's Day, Christmas, Mother's Day, Father's Day, the annual family reunion, their birthday, your birthday, any birthday in the family, the annual winter vacation to sunnier climes, Thanksgiving, Easter, Family Day, the couples get-together you used to attend, parent school nights, long weekends, summer holidays at the cottage, anniversaries and the big one, the deathiversary, or depending on your beliefs, the heaveniversary (okay, neither of those are real words, but they should be) marking the day they died each year.

I read one author who described life as flowing along in water, and the death of a loved one as a huge boulder that drops into the flow. Unprepared for how hard the day can be, you totally smash into the boulder the first year. But every year following you see the boulder on the horizon and do your best to prepare to navigate. Despite your bests efforts you may crash into the boulder again. You can try wearing some protective equipment, so the crash doesn't hurt so much. You can try a different approach as the boulder looms. You can try to jump over it. You can decide to not fight it and sit on it awhile. Every year may be different. What you know for sure is the deathiversary boulder comes every year, and all you can do is your best.

The same can be said for dealing with all those other difficult days. You can see them coming and will need to do something to prepare for them. Remember, it is okay to say no if you don't feel like being with other people on a particular day. Sometimes solitude is better than dealing with your emotions in front of a crowd.

Ideas for the Anniversary of their Death

- Bring a picnic to the cemetery
- Spend a day at the lake or another favoured place of your loved one
- Visit their favorite restaurant and share memories around the table
- Look through some of your loved one's treasures
- Gather some friends to watch videos, including the ones on your loved one's phone
- Do something active like a hike or bike ride in honor of your loved one.

Ideas for the Christmas holidays

- Serve your loved one's favourite meal, meat or vegetable, dessert, cookies or breakfast
- Plan an after-dinner drinks time where everyone can remember and talk about the person who died
- Play your loved one's favourite holiday music, or sing your loved one's favourite holiday song
- Lay out a paper tablecloth and some pens. Encourage family and friends to write down their favourite memory from the past year. Save the tablecloth and bring it out the following year along with a new paper tablecloth
- Light a candle to burn throughout the holidays (you can use a flameless one)
- On Christmas Eve, give everyone an unlit candle. The first person lights their candle and shares a memory, then lights the candle of the next person. You can finish with a prayer or blessing
- Set up a memory stocking or memory box where you and others can write down the memories you treasure, then take some time to read them together
- Allow people to share the name of a loved one they've lost and have a moment of silence to remember them
- Add an extra plate at the table, or set aside a chair to symbolize welcoming their memory into your celebrations
- Invite someone who doesn't have family to the holiday meal
- Put out photos from past holidays on a table
- Find remembrance ornaments and a special tree for them. You may wish a special ceremony to light this tree
- Buy gifts for your loved one on their birthday or Christmas, then donate them to a local hospital or nursing home
- Donate a few hours to your loved one's favourite charity
- Donate a holiday meal through your church or local social services
- Donate altar flowers or other holiday decorations to your place of worship in the name of your loved one
- Splurge on a gift for yourself

Be gentle and kind. You are learning a new way to live.

Grief Stew: Perpetual Card

When a family friend died, his family brought a huge anniversary card to the funeral home. The man who died had been married for decades. He bought this card on their first anniversary. Every year he got the card out and added another year's entry to it. The card was filled with years of love notes to his wife. What a treasure for her to have afterwards.

You can do a similar thing to mark a special day – their birthday, your anniversary, Valentine's Day or the New Year. Find one of those huge cards. Each year add an entry for that year – something you would write if your loved one was still alive. Be sure to date your entries.

Reflection: On Handling the Difficult Days

Page 73 in the Honest Grief Notebook

What was the worst special occasion day? What was your best one? What is the impact of planning ahead? What have you learned from all the special day experiences? Any thoughts on handling future special dates?

Diamond: Remembering Ornament

Craft stores sell clear glass and plastic Christmas tree ornaments. You can add photos and other sentimental things inside and write on the outside. It makes a great remembrance for your Christmas tree. I created a new one each year. If you are unsure, do a search online for inspiration.

Helping Others

When your storms begin to settle, many people find they want to contribute to life in a more meaningful way. You can contribute to a charity or cause you believe in, or help others in need. Consider donating your time to a grief support group. Others facing loss need to know people have forged their own path through grief and have found serenity in their new way of living with the hole in their heart and the missing person in their life.

Think about what you needed in the depths of your grief and be that for someone else. Walk alongside them while they struggle through their dark days.

I've heard it said, "The kindest hearts have felt the most pain." You are now a kind heart.

Be gentle and kind. You are learning a new way to live.

Grief Stew: Pay It Forward

Here are a number of ways you can demonstrate your support to another person grieving. They also might inspire additional creative ways you can show your support.

- Set on your calendar a reminder for your friend's loss anniversaries (1 month, 2 month and so on) and call, email, write, send along a little gift to brighten their difficult days and help them not feel so alone. Consider sharing your memories of their loved one or perhaps memories of times you and your friend enjoyed together
- Set up a fund for their family. This allows people who don't know the family well a way of expressing their support. Your friend can use it to fund a family kindness, like a vacation
- Organize the community to contribute 30 days of meals (food that can be frozen, thawed and reheated), or deliver baked goods like cookies, muffins and scones
- If there are children, bring over a new book, or take the kids to a museum, park or nearby kid-friendly activity
- If you are going to give flowers, consider an orchid. They last a long time
- Bring over a package of teas and things that go with it
- If they have a fire pit or fireplace, deliver some wood, tinder, instant hot chocolate and marshmallows for roasting
- If you know the grieving person well, don't ask, just go do their dishes, get their laundry done, or clean their bathrooms
- Acknowledge their loss and say the name of their loved one. It just feels good to hear someone else say their name
- Give them an anniversary wine gift – a bottle they can open on each anniversary. If you don't live nearby, you could call them up to chat and sip a glass of wine with them
- Plant a tree in memory of their loved one. Be sure to plant it someplace they can visit and water it for them
- Give them a bottle of special liqueur, something they can share with friends and remember
- If you come across a painting, a poem, or music you think fits, send it to them

Reflection: On Giving Back

Page 74 in the Honest Grief Notebook

How does it feel to be a support for others? How do you feel about being on this part of the grief journey? What do you value from this experience?

Thank You

Congratulations. You have come a long way from your moment of loss. You have not abandoned the hard struggle of working through all that goes with a great loss. You are not the person you once were, but you have found a way to live again.

You once were tossed about on the sea of loss, among mountainous waves, but now you've found your way back to land. As you walk the shoreline of life, you may find a grief storm hits when you least expect it. It does for me. And resentment, anger or anguish revisit for a time. And I need to circle back to those exercises that got me through the tough times. Continue to be gentle and kind to yourself. Continue to pursue your place of peace.

Thank you for reading *Honest Grief*. If you've found this book to be beneficial, can you do me a favour? Please leave a review to let others know. You'll be helping other people in grief find a way through their storm, and you'll be helping me too. You can make a big difference. Thank you so much!

About the Author

Serenity McLean grew up in Ontario and moved to western Canada in 2004. She returned to Ontario in 2017. With a Masters degree in Adult Education, she took on various roles at several colleges. She also worked in the Information Technology sector predominantly in project management.

She wrote her first fictional book just before getting laid off in an economic downturn. She took this opportunity to make a career change – committing her time to writing, blogging, and helping others along the path of publication.

She took a hiatus to care for her terminally ill mother and deal with a long series of losses. Born of the pain and sorrow of her grief, and combined with her education background, she wrote Honest Grief as a way to help others facing the hurt of deep losses. The additional pain inflicted by those around her who didn't understand her grief and its deep gaping wounds inspired her to write a companion book, *Supporting Honest Grief* (to be released in 2018). It is written specifically for people who have a grieving friend.

Along with art and photography, Serenity spends her time with her dog. She's enjoyed the sunny disposition of golden retrievers for over thirty years. In the summer months, Serenity and her goldie can be found swimming in the local lakes and relaxing under the sun.

Follow Serenity McLean

Website: http://serenitymclean.com/

Facebook: https://www.facebook.com/Serenityauthor/

Instagram: https://www.instagram.com/serenitymclean_/

Pinterest: https://www.pinterest.ca/mclean3963/

References

Books

Mike Ashcraft and Rachel Olsen, <u>My One Word</u> (Zondervan, 2012).

Susan Cain, <u>Quiet: The Power of Introverts in a World That Can't Stop Talking</u> (Broadway Books, 2013).

Serenity McLean, <u>Honest Grief Notebook</u> (Dometree, 2017). Retrieved from http://serenitymclean.com/honest-grief/

Websites

Envelope Books: Cloth Binding How-To (2017) Retrieved from https://www.marthastewart.com/270217/envelope-books-cloth-binding-how-to

Honest Grief Notebook (2017) Retrieved from http://serenitymclean.com/honest-grief/

How to Make an Accordion Book (2017) Retrieved from http://www.readbrightly.com/diy-accordion-book/

Interactive Star Chart (n.d.) Retrieved from http://www.heavens-above.com/main.aspx

Name a Star Live (2004) Retrieved from https://www.nameastarlive.com

Your Star Map (2017) Retrieved from https://www.thenightsky.com

www.ingramcontent.com/pod-product-compliance
Lightning Source LLC
LaVergne TN
LVHW011202080426
835508LV00007B/555